BLIZZARD

BLIZZARD
1 · 9 · 4 · 9

Roy V. Alleman

The Patrice Press
St. Louis, Missouri

4th printing

**Library of Congress
Cataloging-In-Publication Data**

Alleman, Roy V., 1909-
    Blizzard 1949
        p.   cm.
    ISBN 0-935284-88-5: $9.95
    1. Blizzards—West (U.S.)—History—20th century. 2. West
(U.S.)—History—1948-1950. I. Title
F595.A47   1991
978—dc20   90-25960
                                                                 CIP

Photo credits: 121, *Alliance* [Nebraska] *Times*; 62, Minnilusa Pioneer Museum, Rapid City, So. Dak.; 10, 92, 103, Nebraska State Historical Society, Lincoln; 25, 31, 45, 71, 78, 117, 134, 175, 179, 181, *Omaha World-Herald*; 110, 141, 154, 177, Ed Swopes, Ord, Nebr.; 98, 103, Harold E. Thompson, Gordon, Nebr.; 83, 87, 157, 171, Worley Studios, Alliance, Nebraska, furnished by Castle Corbett; 40, 59, 144, 151, 159, 161, 168, 184, 187, Wyoming History Museum, Cheyenne.

Cover illustration by Lee Brubaker

The Patrice Press
1701 S. Eighth Street
St. Louis MO 63104

Printed in the United States of America

To my wife, Irene

Acknowledgments

It would be impossible to acknowledge all those involved in putting together this book. Yet I feel I must acknowledge as many as I can—especially those thirty persons who wrote offering their experiences of that awful winter. I also appreciate the efforts of the librarians who sent photo copies of newspaper accounts. Kirk T. Mears, county agent at Rapid City, South Dakota, lent me the history he compiled during the storms.

I thank Dr. Dwight Marsh of Hastings College for helping get the book on track, and Irene Abernethy and Joyce Ore, who patiently read galley proofs. But, above all, I thank my wife, Irene, who also read copy and waited (sometimes skeptically) for something to happen; and my daughter, Carol Nowka, who forced me into the computer age. I fought that, but without the computer, this project never would have been accomplished.

Roy Alleman
January 1991

BLIZZARD

1

November 18, 1948 . . .

LIVING ALONG HIGHWAY 96 in west-central Kansas, D. O. Durr poked the fire in her coal-burning stove on this Wednesday morning, then moved to her front window to watch what she felt was a developing storm. The day had begun with a drizzling rain but the wind switched to the north quickly and now flakes of snow slipped sidewise past the window and formed a small drift in her front yard. The balmy morning weather was rapidly becoming cooler. She went to her woodshed to bring in another hod of coal and set it near the stove.

Across the highway stood a large cottonwood tree and a small snowdrift began to form on its leeward side. Nervously, Durr watched the highway traffic, which was unusually heavy with people hurrying to join friends and relatives for the weekend and for the approaching Thanksgiving holiday. She, too, had planned a dinner engagement with friends. She would not be going.

As the day wore on, the storm's intensity increased. The snowdrift in her yard grew larger, as well as the snowdrift near that cottonwood. Contrary to what she had heard on her radio that morning, the snowfall was turning into a full-blown blizzard. As visibility decreased, traffic began to move more slowly. She watched through swirling snow as drivers hit the drift near the cottonwood and stalled, then backed up, revved up the motor and hit it hard enough to get through. But, even if they got through this one, what of the next? This won't be the last snowbank on that desolate highway, she thought.

Weather in western Kansas, as in many western states, can be an outlaw—unpredictable, vicious, and fast changing. Sudden snowstorms are to be expected, as Durr had learned over the years. They were known as "blue northers," a term originated by early-day cowboys because they said a man turned blue from the cold.

Durr wondered if these travellers had overshoes, heavy coats, and blankets in the car in case of emergency. People in warm cars rarely realize what could happen if a car stalled or the engine quit.

Finally, though the increasing snow clouded her view, she saw an auto stop. It backed up and rushed forward, wheels spinning. The driver tried again, hitting the drift again even harder than before. This time, however, the car spun across the road. They're done for now, she said to herself. But so is anyone else who comes down that road. They can't get by.

Durr watched as two people got out of the car and headed for her house. She stepped back from the window so that they would not see her watching.

Soon there came a knock on her front door. She opened it and in front of her stood a young man and woman, he with a small bundle in his arms. The man stomped the snow from his feet and shook it from his light overcoat. The storm whipped snow around them and into the house. She urged them to come in. They introduced themselves as Jim and Janet Smythe.

"We're stuck in the snow," he said, shivering.

Durr hurried to help them unwrap, putting coats over chairs to dry. She helped them to gather around the stove. Janet Smyth opened the bundle and then Durr saw a tiny baby who blinked at the light and whimpered. She was about to scold them for taking such a small child out in such weather when she heard another knock on the door. There stood an elderly man, bracing against the wind and shivering, his heavy wool coat covered with snow. She urged him in.

"I'm stuck in the snow behind another car and can't move either direction," he said, teeth chattering.

Before she could learn more, there was another knock on the door. There stood a man and woman with two children.

Through the storm she could see more cars stop. From then on a stream of people headed for her door. Soon it was a houseful, jammed into every corner, sitting on the floor, leaving the chairs and couches for the elderly. (She learned that the elderly man was ninety years old and was going west to visit a son.) Durr hurried to get chairs from the kitchen, from the dining room and from the bedrooms.

She even brought in from the back porch her dilapidated rocking chair in which she would rock and watch the prairie sunset during the summer.

By this sunset, if one could have seen it through the storm, Durr counted thirty-nine persons of all ages in her modest three-bedroom home. Where would they sleep? How could she feed so many?

Those taken in by Durr were among the lucky ones during this storm which blew in from Oklahoma (so it was said) and tracked across portions of Kansas, New Mexico, Wyoming, South Dakota, and Nebraska. Not many homes had as many guests as Durr had. Far more people were trapped in their cars, huddled in light blankets, many of them lightly clothed.

Within hours roads were closed between Kansas and Colorado. Snowplows sent out to open the roads became stuck. More than one hundred motorists were stranded at Limon, Colorado (pop. 1,800), and had to spend the night in private homes or sleep on cots provided at the First Methodist Church.

Twenty towns in the Republican River Valley in Kansas and Nebraska were isolated and without telephone services. High-speed trains taking Thanksgiving vacationers across the plains east or west were stalled in huge drifts. Passengers suffered but survived when water pipes in stalled engines froze solid.

Trapped on summer ranges, many cattle and sheep died, suffocating in the blizzard even though the weather was not especially cold.

In Hastings, Nebraska, Dorothy June Olson was preparing for her wedding to Billy Gangwish, who lived seven miles to the southwest. It was scheduled for Saturday at 4 P.M. with the Reverend Frank Schroeder officiating. Rehearsal was to be Friday night. Dorothy watched out the window as the slow rain suddenly turned into a blizzard such as she had never seen. She and her mother worked on her wedding dress and kept an eye on the developing storm. They worried about whether Billy could get to town. Dorothy tried to call his home. The operator told her that all lines out of town were down. The snowbank in front of their window was getting higher and higher.

"I've never seen so much snow in my life," said Dorothy June to her mother. "I'm afraid Billy will never make it in by Saturday."

Mark Prichard, on a farm near Spalding in northeast Nebraska, was ready for school. He watched his father, Mark, and two hired pickers hitch horses to their wagons, preparing to harvest a huge corn crop. There was fog in the air. Soon a gentle rain began to fall, then a drizzle. Abruptly it was a roaring blizzard.

"No picking today," said his father. And Mark, Jr., didn't attend school.

C. B. ("Cy") Wolfe of Hastings was an enthusiastic shortwave ham radio operator. So far it had been just a hobby for him, but suddenly his hobby became a vital necessity in the area when the telephone lines went down. He was of no use to Dorothy June, as Billy didn't have a ham radio. He was of more use to the Burlington Northern Railroad, which had a train it could not locate.

The dispatcher called Cy at the *Hastings Daily Tribune*, where he was mechanical superintendent. "Can you help?"

"I'm not sure," replied Wolfe. "We're terribly short of help because so many didn't make it to work. I'll see."

He turned to foreman Dick Batt. "Go ahead," said Batt. "We have to help if some train crew is in trouble."

Wolfe struggled an hour through ever-deepening snow to get home. There he began calling all hams in the area. Finally he got his answer from a fellow ham in Culbertson, some 100 miles southwest of Hastings.

"Yes, the train stalled just west of town," he reported. "The crew hoofed it into town and is safe. It's a freight train."

The newspaper was about to go to press by the time Wolfe made it back. After work he spent most of the night as liaison between other operators in the Republican Valley, reporting to relatives and friends in Hastings. He also became liaison between doctors in Hastings and ill patients in the valley. In fact, Wolfe became such a hero that night the community later gave him an award.

Back in the Durr home, the next order of business was to get everyone fed and settled in for the night. The storm had intensified until there was no way anyone could find a way through it. Those who had not found shelter would have to stay in their cars or perish in the cold and snow.

"How can you feed so many people?" asked the Smythes.

"Don't worry, there's plenty," said Durr. "I have a cellar full of food."

"We'll help," offered the two. So did many others.

The cellar was now buried under snow. Durr and Jim Smythe grabbed a washtub and went out into the howling blizzard. Jim picked up a shovel and scooped a narrow path to the cellar a few feet away, then scooped out the door and opened it. He blinked with disbelief when he surveyed the packed cellar. They loaded the tub with hams, potatoes, and stored vegetables. After carrying in one tubfull, they went back for another of home-canned tomatoes, beans, and fruit.

"We won't starve," laughed Jim.

Other men went to the woodshed, also nearby, and brought in hods full of coal, enough for the night. Jim helped fire up the huge kitchen range, and when it was hot, Durr popped a ham into the oven. Meanwhile some of the women peeled potatoes and filled kettles simmering on the stove with canned beans and tomatos. Durr brought out five large loaves of bread.

''Thought I might have company someday,'' she said, smiling.

The dining room table was set. Durr invited the minister in the group to ask the blessing. Then everyone was invited to fill a plate and find a place to sit.

But where to sleep? Durr brought out all the blankets she had. A few guests had brought in the blankets they had carried in their cars. They decided to sleep in relays in the beds. Some chose to stay up, visit, or play cards. When they could stay awake no longer, they sprawled out on the floor.

Saturday, November 19 . . .

In Hastings things were no better. When the storm finally quit, snowplows pushed out one-lane trails through the streets, and Dorothy June could get to the church. But there was no word from Billy. She waited and waited—and waited. Came 4 P.M. and still no Billy. Dorothy June gave up and went home.

But she had not reckoned with Billy's determination to attend his own wedding. Saturday morning he and his parents dressed in their Sunday best, picked up a couple of scoop shovels, and headed for Hastings. They knew that blizzards have a habit of piling up snow in big mounds and leaving bare spots elsewhere. Also, storms tend to sweep from the north and leave north and south roads fairly clear. Billy and his parents started north up a road, but could find no east-west road open, even though they drove to the county line.

They turned around and drove south, this time to the other end of the county. Still no chance to get east. They drove back to Highway 6 west of Hastings. From there they drove across fields, circling snowbanks, shoveling and driving until they arrived about a mile west of Hastings. Ahead of them was a fifteen-foot drift across the highway. But from there on it looked like a clean sweep into town.

"Don't you think we might as well go home?" suggested Billy's father, Earl. He had been ready to turn back for a long time.

"We've gone this far, we might as well scoop our way through," answered the determined Billy.

Now nearly exhausted, the men began shoveling at what looked like a mountainous drift. Hours later they drove into town, where they found an insurmountable drift. Billy left the car and walked the remaining six blocks to Dorothy June's house.

At 11:30 P.M., Dorothy June heard a knock on the door. There stood Billy, looking like anything but ready for a wedding.

Scene on November 25, 1948, at the Albert Miller farm in Danbury, Nebraska.

"I've been shoveling snow since daylight this morning," said a bushed Billy. "We drove forty miles to get seven."

They called the minister and re-scheduled the wedding for 4 P.M. Sunday. It went off without a hitch, except that there was only a small crowd and there was no wedding cake. Billy's aunt, who had offered to bake it, lived in Holstein thirty miles away and couldn't make it to Hastings. Billy's brother, the best man, taught school in Westerville, Nebraska, eighty miles north. He had been only five minutes late the day before. He had chartered a small plane and flown down.

Seven persons were reported to have died in the

storm. In O'Neill, Nebraska, the pastor of a church told his congregation about Clyde Streeter, who lived eight miles out in the country and who needed to be hospitalized. Two hundred men from the congregation went home, picked up shovels, scooped a path to the ranch, and helped bring Streeter to the hospital for much-needed medical attention.

Then the weather turned warm. Huge snowbanks began to melt and a trail was opened past the Durr home. Suddenly her guests were free to leave.

They volunteered to pay her, but she refused. "Out here we take care of each other," she said. But she did give a sigh of relief as she watched the last car slip out of sight behind a snowbank.

It was already a winter of contrasts. At about the same time this blizzard swept across the western states, a tornado ripped through Warren, Arkansas, killing forty-six and injuring nearly 300. Doctors and nurses from nearby communities, from Hot Springs and from Little Rock, worked through darkness and rain and by lamplight and candlelight, to treat victims. The storm swept through the twenty-block business district, wrecking the industrial and residential areas.

In December the weather turned warm, the snow melted, and ranchers got their herds together and assessed their losses. The railroads again ran on time and high-speed passenger coaches were filled. The good weather led to complacency. Scores of people hopped aboard the trains or got into cars to visit relatives and to celebrate the Christmas and New Year's holidays. There was little thought that the November storm might have been a prelude to something even more severe.

Forecasters saw little in the weather charts to indicate something big might be in the offing. Even after a pre-blizzard drizzle began falling, they saw nothing to indicate more than snow flurries and said so in the morning forecasts. The balmy days felt more like spring.

From Arizona and New Mexico, to Nevada, Utah, Wyoming, the Dakotas, and Nebraska, the next storm began with a light drizzle.

Quickly the rain changed to snow and finally to a blinding blizzard that would completely paralyze this vast portion of the nation. Meteorologists were hard pressed to explain what happened.

The blizzards of 1949 were on their way.

2

January 1, 1949. . .

NEW YEAR'S DAY began as a day everyone likes to see in winter, but seldom does. The sun shone warmly and much of the snow from previous storms had melted. Cattle and sheep were grazing winter range and growing fat. That is, they would grow fat if this weather held for the rest of the winter. Sometimes there were winters like that.

North of Ashby, Nebraska, Gene Thurston and his partner, Lauren Dikes, had given their herds an extra feed of hay and cottonseed cake the day before and had driven their pickup to the Ashby home of Gene and his wife, Pauline, for a rest. Their plan was to enjoy the day with the family and return Monday morning to the Cooley Camp where they batched together and fed their herds.

That morning Gene did what every other rancher and farmer does each morning—he turned on the radio and got the weather report. The announcer, this time from radio station KOA, Denver, predicted another nice day with a possibility of snow flurries. Predicting the weather for the Rocky Mountain and the Great Plains states is not an exact science today; it wasn't then, either. KOA was a powerful station that could be heard for hundreds of miles around. People didn't trust this radio weatherman's report any more than any other report, but ranchers enjoyed his humor. He might say, ''Cowboys, pull your hats down low, there'll be high winds today.'' He did help in decision-making. If he had reported a blizzard, likely Gene's father, Clyde, would have driven those 150 cull cows (crippled or barren animals) to another pasture, away from the lake where he had put them.

Pauline was making plans for a New Year's Day dinner. The boys had missed getting in for Christmas because of a December 23 snowstorm.

Near Cozad, Nebraska, Marvin and Norma Thinnes discussed the approaching birth of their child and whether Norma should move into town to be near the doctor and a hospital. They took a stroll in the noonday sun and decided to wait. There was no serious hint of a storm, either in the cloudless sky or in the weather forecasts coming over their radio.

Dave and Gladys Nordstrom stopped by to chat with my wife, Irene, and me at our farm five miles south of Comstock, Nebraska. They agreed to take our collective children to school the next day. We had joined with a school district across the river and south. It was too far for the children to walk so we exchanged turns taking them.

In southern New Mexico, J. W. Taylor, Southern Pacific Railroad dispatcher, propped his feet on the seldom-used heating stove in the Lordsburg depot, soaked up the sunshine coming through the window, and watched tourists going west for the winter. One car with a Kansas license plate had a tent secured to the top. Perhaps the family was expecting to spend the winter in it.

In St. George, Utah, Antone Prince met with his sheep-rancher friend, Wayne C. Gardner, at a local restaurant. They, too, discussed the nice weather, and the condition of Gardner's winter range seventy miles south. "The sheep are doing very well," Gardner observed.

In Idaho a bus loaded with twelve skiers checked in at the resort in Twin Springs, anticipating an exciting weekend on the slopes. In the evening snow began to fall heavily and soon there was twelve inches of it on the ground.

Joy C. Fairhead and his wife, Lois, ranchers near Merriman, Nebraska, drove to Alliance to spend New Year's Day with her parents, the Howard Lichtys. Stanley Moreland, Joy C.'s cousin, and his fiancee, Joy Lou Nero, who had been visiting the Morelands, accompanied them. There was no hint of a storm in the air, but, just as they sat down to dinner, Joy C.'s father, Joy Fairhead, called. "Come home at once," he said. "I feel there's a bad storm coming."

Snowdrifts were already piling up on the highway where bushes or banks stopped the wind. Joy C. let Stan off at the Moreland place and drove to the family ranch twenty miles beyond Merriman to help his brother, Garould, gather the herds into the most protected windbreaks and shed. By then it was snowing quite hard.

After a noon dinner Bob Moreland lay down for a nap. When he awoke late in the afternoon he looked out to see a dark, ominous cloud forming in the northwest. A few flakes of snow clung to the window screen. Bob went to bed early, planning to start for the Green Valley Ranch first thing in the morning.

Ruby Stufft and family, who ranched thirty-five miles south of Ainsworth, Nebraska, were busy packing the pickup truck. She and son Harold were to take daughters Evelyn and Vera to their apartment in Ainsworth, where they attended high school. Daughter Dorothy was to take the train to Lincoln where she attended the University of Nebraska.

The weather was fine, but a few flakes of snow fell as they drove out of the yard. The roads were still snow-packed from earlier storms. Ruby, who kept records for the U. S. Weather Bureau, had reported twenty-seven inches of snow in November and another seventeen inches in December. At the last minute, Harold put two shovels in the truck.

January 2, 1949 . . .

Stan Moreland stared at the Ford pickup buried in snow to the top of its fenders.

"Dang it, now what do we do?" he asked his brother Bob, who had just tried to ram through the auto gate on Jay Cole's ranch. The storm was whipping more snow over the top of the vehicle and visibility was nearing zero. They had left their ranch home near Merriman in northwestern Nebraska early that morning in blowing snow, trying to reach their Green Valley Ranch twenty miles northwest. They still had five hopeless miles to go.

Bob did not answer at once. He looked out over the prairie where the snow, pushed by high winds, was rushing across the country like a mad river bursting through a levee. He pulled the sheepskin collar of his heavy wool coat up around his chin and turned his back into the wind to catch his breath.

"Anyway, we won't need this pickup," shouted Bob over the noise of the wind. "It may be here a long time, judging by the way this storm is shaping up. Our only hope of getting to the ranch is to get saddle horses from Cole. We can't walk in this wind."

"Then let's go!" shouted Stan impatiently.

They stumbled up the long driveway to the Cole ranch, pausing frequently to turn and catch their breath, breath sucked away by the howling wind.

Bob Moreland on Comanche, who saw him through the blizzard of 1949.

Often they peeked ahead to be sure they hadn't missed the house and become hopelessly lost. They had a healthy respect for western blizzards.

They had struggled through drifts of snow all morning, trying to reach the upper ranch. The fate of 500 head of cattle hinged on their reaching the ranch headquarters quickly. Payment for the newly purchased ranch depended on their taking good care of this herd. In fact, all their cattle were at this ranch; only a milk cow and a few bulls remained at the home ranch. It had taken them hours to get fifteen miles. How long would it take to get five miles without the benefit of a road?

When they reached the house at last, Jay Cole invited them in. "How about a couple of horses and saddles?" asked Bob.

"Sure, you can have horses, but they're out in the horse pasture," said Jay. "Better stay for dinner first, though, and get warm."

The men refused, wanting to get to their cattle as quickly as possible. By the time Bob had gathered some groceries, Stan had the horses saddled. They spent valuable time assessing where to go, since the trail was completely covered. "Let's take that fence line. I think we can get there if we stay with it," decided Stan.

Fourteen thousand acres of rangeland lay in front of them under mounds of snow and not much was visible to guide them. Their eyes iced over before they had gone a quarter of a mile. White spots appeared on their wrists where sleeves and mittens didn't quite meet. Their horses tried to turn back instead of facing into the blizzard.

When the animals bogged down in the growing drifts, the men got off and let them lunge their way out. Often they had to backtrack to find another way around a drift too deep to navigate. They dared not lose sight of that fence line, even though it meant they would travel much farther than five miles to reach the ranch. Every few minutes they turned their backs to the wind to catch their breath and let their eyes thaw out. It was becoming increasingly harder to breath.

By the time they came in sight of the Green Valley Ranch buildings, both men and beasts were exhausted. Although it was below freezing, the horses were lathered with sweat. Their winter coats were too warm for this struggle.

The men put the horses in the barn and gave them an extra feed of oats. The animals shook so violently and looked so dragged out that Bob grabbed a gunny sack and gave each a rubdown.

He let a few of their horses into the barn and then went into the house for more layers of clothing and to call home to their parents, the Jack Morelands, to tell them they had arrived safely.

A much relieved mother could say only, ''Thank God you're both safe!''

The men rubbed snow on their faces to ease the pain of frostbite, as was the custom of the time, mounted their horses, and went out to check the cattle. They found forty-one yearlings in front of the 150-foot shed, just where the men thought they would be. They had been watered and fed there for nearly a week, so they were content to stay put.

The previous Saturday Joy Fairhead had gone with Bob ''to cake.'' (This entailed giving the cattle a protein supplement. The name derived from the time when cattle were fed cottonseed cakes shipped in from the South.) While Bob was showing his uncle the new corrals he was building, he decided to open a gate that would allow the 244 cows to leave the meadow to find better shelter in case a storm came up.

Fortunately, the cows did find the gate and were in the shelter of a small grove of willows when Bob and Stan found them in the midst of the storm. The men drove them to a corral in front of the shed and then rode the south fence of the meadow to see if they had missed any.

After this, they rode back through the tree lot south of the meadow where 185 calves were bunched up in front of a board windbreak which was south of a cottonwood grove. While they considered the calves well protected, they thought of the possibility of their leaving the windbreak and decided to corral them. This project took an hour. They could drive the calves out a few yards from the grove, but as soon as they were headed into the wind, they turned back. Finally, sensing there might be better shelter ahead, they made a dash for the corral. There Bob and Stan put them in a shed in front of the windbreak and granary. Eleven cows with young calves and six bulls were put into another shed. With their minds much relieved, the men went back to the house to fix coffee and fry steaks.

Rubbering (listening in) on the neighborhood telephone party line, Bob learned that the neighborhood was in much confusion. No one was getting his cattle fed. Most of their neighbors' cow herds were a long way from headquarters, and, by now, the storm was so bad that it was impossible to do anything for them. The Snyders, to the east, had been trying to drive 300 calves from a meadow a mile and a half south of their headquarters up the valley to the protection of a stackyard, but finally had to settle for driving them into a range of hills on the west of that valley. Others reported similar troubles and were worried that heavy losses would result.

After dinner, in spite of the blizzard raging outside, Bob and Stan decided to try feeding the cattle in a stackyard a quarter of a mile away. They harnessed four draft horses and dug out the drag feed sled from under the snow. Then they managed to cable on and feed two loads of hay, which they pitched off in big piles in front of the windbreaks. Cattle on all sides kept the hay from blowing away.

Stan turned on the radio during supper and learned that the weatherman had caught up with the weather. The announcer said they could expect on the morrow "high winds, more snow, and colder weather."

Toward evening, climbing over ever-mounting drifts, the men fought their way to the corrals for a final check on the cattle.

"I guess they're about as well off as possible," Bob commented.

"We've done all that we can. We'll just hope for the best," answered Stan.

Back in the house they checked on their sore spots. Stan's wrists had water blisters where the skin had frozen and turned black. Bob's face was swollen from freezing and had several black spots as well. The men looked at each other and laughed.

"This sure doesn't help my looks any, does it?" chuckled Bob.

Bob put salve on their frostbite and wrapped Stan's wrists. They went to bed wondering what tomorrow might bring.

The next morning a bright sun poured in through the kitchen window of the Thurston home near Ashby, Nebraska. Pauline poured another cup of coffee for her husband, Gene, and neighbor Lauren Dikes. An announcer on the radio mentioned that a storm might be brewing.

"I missed getting home for Christmas and now it looks as if I'll have to hurry back to the cow camp," grumbled Gene. "How about coming with us, Pauline? You could do some housecleaning and take inventory for the tax assessor. We could leave the children with your sister Alma."

Gene and Lauren were feeding cattle at the Cooley Camp some seventeen miles north of Ashby in the middle of the Nebraska Sandhills, a highly developed cattle range that comprises roughly one-fourth of the state. Gene was feeding 850 head for his parents, the Clyde Thurstons, who lived south of the camp a few miles. Dykes was feeding 400 head for Alfred Castle. They batched together at the camp which was, in reality, a small house, once the home of an early-day homesteader.

It was decided that, after a couple of days at the camp, Pauline would return to town and bring out a load of groceries, veterinary supplies, fuel, and other items. There was still snow on the ground from the mid-November storm—bothersome, but not enough to be a problem for experienced cowmen such as Gene and Lauren.

The stores were not open in Ashby, so they tossed a few groceries into the pickup from their own cupboards, put in bedding and a change of clothing, plus a new gas lantern. The children were dropped off at Pauline's sister's home and the three headed north. It was now snowing quite hard.

At the Thurston ranch they stopped to put on tire chains. The snow was getting tough to buck and things didn't look good. Gene talked over the situation with his father.

"Dad, don't you think we should move those thin cows out of the Hibbeler Meadow? They could drift onto the lake in a storm!"

"Oh, I think they'll be all right until morning," his father said.

At the Cooley Camp, Pauline helped Gene hitch four horses to a haysled. The cattle hadn't been fed since the day before. Lauren hitched his sled and went on his way. He didn't have far to go, but Gene had to travel a mile north, around a lake. Gene backed

A cowboy rounds up his bulls during a lull in the blizzard. Many animals were lost.

up the horses to the cart, hooked onto the haysled, and he and Pauline left with snow swirling about them. The storm was such by now that they began to wonder if they should have even started out.

They pulled up to a stack, dragged the cable around it, and pulled on a load. By the time they had forked off this hay to the hungry cattle, the storm was in full progress. And it was getting dark.

"I think we're in for a good one!" Gene shouted. "Let's head back. We can save time by cutting across the lake on the ice."

This was a mistake. The horses floundered and

struggled and fell on the ice and snow, slowly making it across the lake. They did not save time. They came upon a haystack, which they could barely see in the wind and snow.

"We're lost," said Gene. "We don't know where we are or where the house is. Let's turn the horses loose and crawl into that haystack."

"No, we'd just freeze to death," objected Pauline.

They huddled in the cart, trying to find directions or landmarks. There was a slight lull in the blizzard. "Hey, isn't that a light out there?" yelled Pauline. "I can see something swaying in the wind. Let's head for it!"

They kept following that flickering light as the horses struggled more and more in the deepening snow. The horses, with their homing instinct still intact, seemed to want to go that way. They came to a gate which they recognized as one near the house.

Going through it, they continued toward the light. And, there it was, hanging on the windmill near their house: the new gas lantern. Apparently Lauren hung it there to guide them home.

They turned the horses in to the corral and struggled to the house where they literally fell inside, exhausted. Lauren had a big fire going in the old cook stove, the only heat source in the house.

"Did the lantern help you find your way?" asked Lauren.

"You better believe it did. It saved our lives!"

replied Pauline. "We were lost before we saw that light."

The two were much nearer to succumbing to the storm than they realized. Pauline's overshoes and scarf had been almost beaten off her body. Her hands, face, and feet were frozen, and so were Gene's. The snow had packed so tightly around his coat collar that the back of his neck was frozen as well. For several hours they sat numb and dazed, too tired to move, as they slowly thawed out.

When Pauline was able to move about, she looked over the house more closely, since it might be their home for some time. It looked even smaller than she thought at first. She noted one bed, one cot, the cook stove and cupboard, a table and a couple of chairs— enough, maybe, for two bachelors. For three people, no. She scouted the cupboard for something to fix for supper. There wasn't much, even when she included the items she had brought along.

The three had arrived at the house just in time. The storm turned even more violent and raged on all through the night. They pulled blankets over their backs to shut off some of the numbing cold that pervaded the room, and fired up the stove. Throughout the night they burned on one side, froze on the other.

High on the tableland southwest of Chadron, Nebraska, ranchers are used to violent weather, blizzards included. Storms like the one that blew in the night before were not unexpected. But the fury of it on Monday made Benton Marshall and his sons wonder if this would be worse than usual.

"Everyone who has ever moved away from this tableland says winters elsewhere are mild by comparison," remarked Benton to sons Bob and Gene as they stood in the shelter of the barn door, preparing to feed their scattered herds of beef cattle.

Bob pulled his sheepskin coat collar a little tighter as he tied a scoop shovel behind the saddle of his horse. "Not hard to agree with that statement. I'm already predicting this will be a 'bellringer.' I can feel it in my bones," he said.

Gene tied a scoop shovel behind his saddle, too. Ranchhand Lyle Stone was busy harnessing horses with which he and Benton would feed the cattle around headquarters. Bob and Gene were to head for the herds away from the ranch. Each stalled, reluctant to face the white mass of snow beating down on the landscape. Then Bob mounted his horse and Gene did likewise. Their first stop would be the Stec pasture where forty calves were supposedly sheltered in an open-front shed.

The day before in spring-like weather, they had tried to attend church services at the Open Bible Church seven miles away. But no one else had come and they returned home. Feeling that a storm was coming, Benton had insisted, against their "no work on Sunday" policy, that they prepare for the worst by getting everything in shape around the ranch. Bob even greased the wheels of a hayrack which would soon be buried under snow so deep it would not be seen again the rest of the winter.

As Bob and Gene headed for the cattle, the horses lost their footing in the deep snow and went down. Getting up again, they plunged into drifts from which they couldn't free themselves. Time after time the men had to shovel the horses out. Often it looked almost impossible to go on.

At the Stec place, their first stop, Bob and Gene found the forty heifer calves completely sealed in the old straw shed. They scooped out the door and rolled a few bales of hay to them, then rode on to the Anderson Canyon a half mile south. Blizzard winds had blown a bare spot for the cull cows and older cows stationed there. They managed to get a few bales of hay to the animals huddled against a steep bank. One cow was marooned away from the rest of the herd. The brothers tried to scoop her out, but the wind blew the snow back as fast as they could move it away from her.

"Might as well forget her," said Bob. "Likely she won't be our only loss this winter."

Moving on to the school section, they managed to get some hay to the cattle there. But the storm was getting so bad that, if they got ten feet apart, they couldn't see each other. Talking above the howling storm became impossible.

Bob's horse, Comanche, was shod all around but when he went down in a snow drift, the shoes on his back hooves often caught on the front hooves, cutting them severely. Bob got out his fencing pliers, which he always carried on his saddle, and pulled off the rear shoes.

"Let's go home!" shouted Bob above the roar of the storm. Gene nodded approval.

The ride home was tough, even harder than the trip out. The snow whirled around them in a mass, blinding them and sealing their eyes. Each man wiped the snow from his eyes and the rest of his face, trying to see where they should go. Although they tried to pick their route carefully, the horses fell helpless so often the men gave up and dismounted, walking and leading their mounts the rest of the way home.

They stopped on the leeward side of a haystack for a brief rest and some respite from the blizzard. Gene suggested crawling into the haystack for the night. Bob vetoed that idea. "We would freeze."

They plunged on into the white wilderness. Though they were exhausted, there was no rest after they returned to the shelter of the barn at home. Barn doors and the corral were drifted over. They had to scoop a path away from the barn doors before they could put their horses away.

"One thing's for sure, tomorrow likely will be worse," said Bob as they put their saddles away.

Ranches in the Great Plains were blanketed by several feet of snow that stayed for weeks.

In western Nebraska, between Scottsbluff and Kimball, a car carrying Kenneth Hopkins, his wife, and their children became stuck in a snowbank that evening. They had stopped shoveling long enough to catch their breath. It looked hopeless and they had to find shelter soon. The children, though wrapped in blankets, were crying from the cold.

Then came a slight lull in the wind. Kenneth thought he saw a light in the distance. "Hon, isn't that the Hull Church yard light?" he asked his wife.

"If it is, it's the answer to my prayers," she answered. "But who would turn on the church light?"

"Let's go for it, it's our only hope."

Country churches are not plentiful in thinly settled Banner County. But here was one at the right place at the right time. The Hopkinses wrapped the children in blankets and headed for it. They floundered through the snow and wind. When they reached the church, they learned the reason for the miracle of the light. The Wallace Greathouse family, also caught in the storm, had stopped moments earlier at the church for shelter. "We thought it might show someone else the way," said Greathouse. "And so we turned on the yard light."

"Thank you," said Hopkins. "We would have frozen to death in the car. We were lost."

Greathouse had the big stove going full blast and the coal hods filled for the night. The parents tucked the five children under two blankets to keep warm and laid them on the Sunday School table to sleep. A few feet from the stove, water froze.

Snow crept in through every little crack in the door and around the windows. The adults sat and shivered with their coats on and continued to stoke the fire. The children awoke late in the evening, cold and in need of a bathroom. Kenneth found clean cans in the storeroom and that took care of that problem. But there was nothing to eat.

"Maybe, if the storm eases, we can walk over to Ralph Noyes' home for groceries," suggested Kenneth. "But he's a bachelor and won't have much on hand.''

In Cheyenne, Wyoming, John Gillis boarded a bus headed for Denver Monday morning. Like everywhere else before the blizzard hit, the day was beautiful and there was no hint of a storm in the forecast. But twenty miles out of Cheyenne it hit ''with a roar and a holler,'' as Gillis described it. Before long the bus was making about ''five to ten yards per hour.''

Said Gillis: ''The wind shrieked with the most God-awful wail I have ever heard. I began to get a tight feeling in the pit of my stomach. Driving along toward Denver we picked up several motorists marooned in snowbanks. They were done for. Women were crying and men were desperate for help. A few minutes later we were almost stalled, too. By now we were in northern Colorado.

''Sometime later we saw a light and managed to pull in front of the Rockport Inn. The driver kicked open the door and out we jumped. In two steps I was about blind from the wind-driven snow. I stumbled through drifts over my knees and fell flat on my face. This happened four times before I made the door of the tavern. . . .''

Rockport was hardly a town. Count a few houses and the tavern and that was about it. But 465 persons were caught there in the storm, including Gillis. Two hundred of them stayed at the tavern and the rest stayed in the two stalled buses. The snow piled so deep around the buses they had to use windows for doors, but no one dared to get out except for the most ''urgent'' reasons and then only in groups of two or more.

In St. George, Utah, Sheriff Antone Prince paced the floor in his office and worried about his good friend, Wayne C. Gardner, who, that morning, told him he was headed for his sheep camp in the Pigeon Breaks region to take supplies to his herders. It is desert country and snow was all but unheard of. Sheep usually could graze the year around without benefit of hay. Sheepherders often basked in the warm sun while watching their flocks. But now that land was buried under snowdrifts. Prince thought that as soon as the storm ended he would ask his pilot to fly over that range and see if Gardner had made it.

Still further south, J. W. Taylor, Southern Pacific train dispatcher, looked out of his office window in disbelief. Something like this didn't happen in southern New Mexico. A blizzard was threatening to bury the window in front of him. This was supposed to be warm desert country where northerners came to soak up sunshine while those at home froze. There was no sunshine this day.

Reports coming over his telephone and telegraph lines told him this was no delusion. Several trains were stalled in the snow and people in 300 autos, some of them northern snowbirds, were stranded along the highway west of town. Generous people along the way were opening their homes to travelers, with two to ten strangers settled in nearly every home.

Farther west, in Duncan, Arizona, twelve inches of snow had piled up. Highway traffic was stopped but the trains continued to run. In one twenty-mile stretch, a train picked up 200 stranded motorists and was letting them off along the way where local people aided them in finding shelter and food.

Taylor filed a telegraph report: ''This is the finest exhibition of generosity I have ever seen. Snow is knee-deep and road cuts are drifted full. I don't see how we could have coped without the town's citizens' help.''

And, again, in Seneca, Nebraska, in Cheyenne, Wyoming, and across South Dakota, trains stalled in snowdrifts.

The fury of the first snowfall of the Blizzard Winter of 1949 was in progress.

3

January 2. . . (continued)

FIREMAN, V. L. MUNGER, and John ("Dutch") Rogers, railroad engineer, stood outside the depot beside their big steam engine in Ravenna, Nebraska, discussing their chances of success in getting through to Alliance, 300 miles northwest. A storm was already in progress at Alliance, a main terminal. Most of the trip would be through the Sandhills, a thinly settled range country.

"The train dispatcher there isn't sure we should start," said Rogers. "There's a full-blown blizzard in progress there and he's halted all trains. I told him we could make it and he agreed to let us go ahead."

Snow was falling gently. Nothing to get excited about, thought Munger. Still, he felt a nervous tension that was hard to explain. He checked the thermometer again. It was headed down. Quite a change from the balmy day before, when the temperature had been in the sixty-degree range. Now it was down to fifteen degrees and falling. So was the barometer.

"How many passengers?" Rogers asked Tom Griffith, the conductor.

"Twenty-three."

"Pretty light. Maybe that's why they're letting us go ahead. We're mainly a freight train this trip."

The crew also included brakeman Ollie Kuhn and a postal worker whom Munger did not know. Munger checked the thermometer and barometer again. Rogers knew he was stalling.

"If we're going, let's get started," said Rogers, a little impatiently.

Munger and Rogers climbed into the cab. Rogers pulled back gently on the throttle and Munger could feel the surge of power under them. They were on their way. Engines had become so large and powerful that engineers felt nothing could stop the roaring behemoths.

Munger knew from past experience that blizzards came with little or no warning. He checked the water and coal twice. He knew a successful trip through the Sandhills would depend on how well he managed these two essential items.

The wind picked up and snow seemed heavier as they whisked past the villages of Litchfield, Ansley, and Berwyn. At Broken Bow, fifty miles along, Munger replenished the water and coal. At the depot there he noted a minus five degrees on the thermometer. At Anselmo, twenty miles farther and at the eastern edge of the Sandhills range country, the snowstorm was gaining momentum. Drifts two to three feet deep were appearing in road cuts. Rogers stopped in Anselmo to call ahead.

"Fifteen degrees below zero at Halsey and the agent says that no more trains are leaving Alliance. Maybe we should have stayed in Ravenna," said the engineer grimly.

Halsey is halfway to Seneca, the next terminal. Rogers learned from the agent in Halsey that the trains due to meet there were tied up at Seneca trying to thaw water pipes and were already three hours late.

Bucking drifts slowed them considerably now. When Rogers saw a drift ahead he opened the throttle and rammed it at fifty miles per hour. Often, by the time they got through, they were hardly moving. They arrived at Seneca five hours behind schedule. Munger filled the water tank and added more coal, then the crew went to Ruby's Cafe for sandwiches and coffee.

"These sandwiches might have to last a while," said Rogers.

Snow in the road cuts got deeper as they progressed toward Whitman, some seventy miles from their destination. There Munger took on more water and coal and was told theirs was the only train on the track between Ravenna and Alliance. Drifts were now ten to fifteen feet high and the thermometer at Whitman had slipped to minus twenty-eight degrees.

Near Ashby, halfway to Alliance from Whitman,

they came to a drift ten feet deep and one-fourth mile long. High winds were whipping the drift higher and higher. Rogers pulled the throttle all the way back as he let go with a loud curse. He hit the drift at full throttle.

"This may be where we sit!" hollered Rogers.

Munger caught himself pushing on the floor with his feet, like he used to do when his Model T Ford got stuck in the sand. At the end of this drift, the engine was barely moving and the big drive wheels had started to spin.

"We made it!" yelled back Munger.

"Yeah, by the skin of our teeth!"

At Ashby Munger found the water tank frozen. There would be no more water from here to Alliance.

"Now we'll be hard pressed to make it all the way," he told Rogers. "In fact, we can call ourselves lucky if we do."

Rogers mumbled something under his breath and opened the throttle so suddenly the wheels spun on the ice-covered rails. Munger and Rogers were now soaking wet from condensation in the cab and their clothing was beginning to freeze. Seeing a long drift ahead, Rogers pulled the throttle all the way open. Again the huge engine responded with the mighty surge of power for which it was known. Again they hit the drift at fifty miles per hour. It was over seven feet deep and a half-mile long. At the end of the drift the train was barely moving.

An ice-covered locomotive struggled to keep moving through seemingly endless storms.

"Whew!" Roger exclaimed.

Munger let go with a war whoop. "If we hadn't made this one, this is where we would have camped for the rest of the storm!" shouted Rogers over the noise of the blizzard. "We'll make it to Lakeside now," he added, with more confidence.

In this flat country, winds were whipping the tracks clear. By the time they reached Lakeside, a few miles out of Alliance, visibility was reaching zero. The men poked holes through the snow in front of the windows in order to see at all.

As they neared the Lakeside depot Rogers snorted

with dismay. "There's a red board hanging out! We might have made it if he hadn't stopped us."

Rogers scrambled through waist-deep drifts. The order was waiting: "Tie up here with your passengers and crew."

Rogers called Alliance. "We have enough water and coal to get there if we don't make any more stops," he told them.

"Come on in," came back from Alliance. But now the snow was packed so hard beneath the engine it could not move. Rogers rolled back and forth several times before the engine began to inch forward. Munger felt like kissing it.

The blizzard was hammering at them full blast now. Rogers strained to see through the blowing snow as darkness moved in. Most of the time he could see nothing. At Birdsall, a section station between Lakeside and Alliance, they hit another long cut filled with snow. Again Rogers barely made it through.

"How about water?" he asked Munger.

"We'll make it," Munger assured him, but he didn't say he was nearly out of coal.

On the flats east of Alliance the blizzard zoomed in with winds of fifty miles per hour. Snow sifted in through every little crack in the cab. The engine stalled in a fifteen-foot drift about 100 yards from the Alliance depot.

"Will this do?" asked Rogers with a grin.

"Suits me fine," said a much-relieved Munger. It

was the first time he had taken a deep breath since leaving Ravenna. He checked the water once more. The tank was empty. The big, faithful engine was beginning to cool.

The section crew hopped out immediately, shoveling a path for the passengers who hurried gratefully to the depot and the nearby hotel.

It would be January 15 before another train would leave Alliance in either direction.

Back in Seneca, halfway between Broken Bow and Alliance, the train crews were not so lucky. A troop train was stalled with frozen water pipes. So were two other trains—200 passengers in all. While they struggled, the snow got deeper and deeper on the north side of a bluff west of town. By the time the pipes were thawed out, the snow was so deep at this bluff there was no chance of moving ahead. Munger and Rogers were the last to get through.

Passengers gathered together and shared the few blankets they had plus those from the Pullman coaches, but they continued to get colder and colder. Finally, late that night, the conductor gave the order to leave the train and make a dash for Ruby's Cafe, the only restaurant in this town of less than 200. It boasted of one hotel.

Passengers were ordered to move ahead on the train and leave from the forward coach. By keeping close to the remaining cars and the engine on the leeward side, it was possible to walk unaided. Beyond the engine was open space. Snow cascaded down, driven by hurricane-force winds and, for the 100-yard space remaining between passengers and the cafe, the men had to steady the women. Even so, both men and women fell often as they staggered through the raging storm.

Passenger William Adams had been trying to keep comfortable a sick passenger who seemed to have pneumonia. Adams, assisted by two other men, helped the ill man to the cafe, sometimes carrying him through the snow. Inside, they brought him to a corner near the stove and covered him with blankets. He weakly gave his name as Orville Miller of Lincoln, Nebraska. Adams called out for a doctor but there was none.

''This man is very ill,'' said Adams. ''He needs medical attention.''

He learned of a Dr. P. H. J. Carothers in Broken Bow, but there was no way for him to get to Seneca. In spite of the number of hungry guests, the cook brought a big bowl of hot chicken soup to alleviate Miller's chills.

Adams put in a call to Dr. Carothers. The soup is fine, the doctor said, and then suggested a few other remedies such as might be found in a Seneca cafe. ''I'll come up as soon as a train runs,'' said the doctor. ''That's the best I can do. This town is already snowed in.''

Others also did the best they could to keep the sick

man comfortable. One man laid his fur coat over Miller who thanked him through labored breaths.

The other passengers ate when they could, lay down wherever they could, and made the best of the situation. Waitresses stayed on duty through the night simply because there was no way home through the snowstorm.

The guests fared so well largely because Bill McCreath, the cafe owner, had just filled his meat cooler with beef. Many stranded passengers ate steak that night.

Nebraska was not the only state with stalled trains. Fifty trains were reported stalled between Pocatello, Idaho; Salt Lake City; and Omaha, Nebraska. Many of them were high-speed transits, such as the City of Los Angeles, the City of Denver Zephyr and one simply called the Utahn. These were the preferred means of transportation of the day, moving across the nation at eighty to ninety miles per hour with short stops along the way. They furnished full comfort en route with high-class restaurants and luxurious Pullman cars.

However, feeling unstoppable that night, trainmen rushed through drifts until they were dead on the tracks, their engines buried under mountains of snow or halted by frozen water pipes.

Trains were stopped at the most unlikely places. The City of Denver Zephyr stalled at Nunn, Colorado, where the town of 150 saw its population more than

Two locomotives trying to open the Burlington Railroad line near O'Neill, Nebraska, gave up the fight.

double overnight. Passengers stayed aboard the train until the heat was cut off. Then the local citizens stepped in. There was no way for the town's little cafe to handle so many people, so residents took them into their homes.

By the evening of January 3, 4,000 people were stranded in Wyoming in trains, autos, and buses. One thousand of them were trapped aboard six east-bound Union Pacific trains near Green River, Wyoming (pop. 13,000).

Fifteen miles south of Arnold, Nebraska, Ron Loebig gunned the motor of his frozen food truck once more. It moved not an inch.

"We're stuck." He really didn't have to tell his travelling companion, Wiley Ferguson, who also knew they were stuck. The blizzard blasting away outside told them they might be here for a while if they didn't find shelter.

"If I'm correct, there's a farmhouse not far from here," said Ron. "Let's tie ourselves together and try to reach it."

Ron found a light rope in the truck, tied himself to Wiley, and they started out in a storm that had reduced visibility to near zero. Ron hunted for a certain fence line he remembered and then a farmyard gate that should be near at hand. When he felt the gatepost he looked up to see the outline of a house.

They stumbled over more snowbanks to reach the house which, fortunately, was open, thanks to a ranchland custom of leaving houses unlocked. Inside they peeled off their wraps and overshoes and started one fire in the cook stove and another in the base burner in the dining room.

Loebig wondered if he should have been so conscientious about giving his customers such good service. When someone in Arnold had called him at Kearney, telling him they were in need of frozen food, he decided to go. Wiley, a wrestler, offered to accompany him. Those long stretches of open prairie north of the Platte River made Ron nervous when the weather was bad. Snow was blowing when they left Gothenburg and by ten miles out, it had turned into a blizzard.

Listening on the party telephone line, Ron learned

that the owners of the house, Mr. and Mrs. Harry Estle, were snowed in at Omaha. A helpful neighbor called the Estles, who in turn called their house.

"Help yourself to what's there," Estle told Ron, "and would you do the chores?"

"Sure." Ron learned the chores consisted of feeding a herd of cattle, a pen of hogs, and a flock of chickens. It wasn't a bad trade.

That evening they fed the chickens, cattle, and hogs, and gathered the eggs. For supper Ron fried eggs and balanced the meal with canned goods hauled up from a nearby cave. The blizzard continued in full force.

"We might be have to settle in for a long haul," he told Wiley. He investigated the bookshelves and magazine rack, and turned on the radio. After learning they were in the middle of a major storm which was attacking much of the West, he called the mayor of Arnold.

"We're snowed in at the Estle ranch," he told him. "And it looks as if we'll be here a long time. There's no way to get out."

"As soon as it clears we'll send out a crew with a snowplow," said the mayor. "Grocery stocks here are already low."

A few miles south of Loebig's truck, Merton and Opal Thompson's car stalled in a drift on the same road. Snow driven under the hood had dampened the distributor and the motor was dead.

"This is where we'll weather the storm," Merton

told his wife. "Let's get as comfortable as we can." Merton pulled the seatcovers off the front seat while Opal slipped into a pair of slacks which one of their daughters had sent back with them for washing. They fastened a sheet over the windows to shut out the cold. Then they climbed in the back seat, wrapped up in the blanket they always carried in winter, and sat on their feet.

"We're going to get awful cold anyway," said Merton. "We should have stayed with the girls in Curtis."

The Thompsons, who lived near Anselmo some sixty miles north, had delivered their two daughters to the Agricultural High School at Curtis. They might have gotten closer to home had they not stopped in Gothenburg to look for Opal's brother who was supposed to have come there seeking work. He was not to be found and so they started north on the Arnold road.

The Thompsons did not know that the temperature had dropped to minus six degrees. They slapped and rubbed their bodies to improve blood circulation. As night came they resorted to talking and telling jokes to keep each other awake. To fall asleep might bring death.

"Remember when we starched that neighbor's underwear?" laughed Merton. "Or how we frosted cupcakes with Ex-Lax for another neighbor?"

"He still won't eat cupcakes," giggled Opal.

"Remind me to burn our *Farmer's Almanac* when

we get home. It predicted warm, balmy days ahead,''
added Merton.

After a while it seemed to be warmer in the car.
The windows became strangely dark. ''I know why.
We're buried in snow,'' Merton decided.

Harriet Brown, 100 years of age and a former slave,
lived in Gordon, Nebraska. During the blizzard she
opened the door of her small home to watch the storm.
Unable to close it, she froze to death. Near Rockport,
Colorado, Philip Roman, his wife, and two children
died trying to walk one mile to a farm home after their
car stalled in a drift.

Andy Archuleta and his wife were within one mile
of their home when their Ford stalled in a drift. It appeared (when they were found) that he had taken off
a hubcap, rounded up a fence post, and then tried to
start a fire in the hubcap. The couple froze to death.

A man, his wife, and their four-year-old daughter
were taking hogs to Denver. Their truck stalled in the
snow. He tried to walk for help and perished. His wife
and daughter stayed in the truck and survived.

The storm had turned murderous.

4

January 3. . . .

THE HOWL OF THE BLIZZARD intensified through the night at the Moreland ranch near Merriman, Nebraska. It shook the house and rattled the windows. Snow seeped in through the smallest cracks around the windows and doors. Bob and Stan's father, Jack Moreland, had called the night before and warned Bob that it would be worse the next day. It certainly was. Visibility was nearly zero. Stan had brought two shovels to the kitchen the night before, knowing that they would have to shovel their way out of the house the next morning. At daylight he was up, bringing out the bacon and coffee. He began mixing the pancake batter on the kitchen table.

Bob opened the front door to look at the storm. The force of the wind almost jerked the door from his hand. A flurry of snow struck him in the face and spread across the floor.

"Can you see the barn, Bob?" called Stan.

"I can't even see the end of the porch!" Bob replied.

In the living room Bob found a bushel of snow that had blown in through a crack in the door. He thought it looked pretty, like a small pyramid. He scooped it out the door and a swoosh of snow followed him back in.

Bob bundled up, went outside, and tried to follow the yard fence to the corrals. The top of the fence posts were still sticking a little above the snow. There he found the cattle huddled together with two inches of caked snow all over them. Their eyes were frozen shut and chunks of ice the size of quart jars hung from their noses. He floundered from one lot to another, finding gates completely covered and drifts twelve feet high. The windbreak where they had put the calves was all but drifted full.

Bob's first concern was to determine how many calves were under those drifts. He counted as best he could through the blinding wind and snow and came up forty to fifty short. He rammed a crowbar into the sides of the drifts expecting to strike calves. Nothing.

Then he staggered back to the house, plunging through waist-deep swirling, blinding snow. Ice particles cut his sore face as he struggled to stay on course. He felt as if he had already done a day's work and he hadn't even had breakfast yet.

After breakfast the two men went back to inventory the cattle and to water and feed the horses. They agreed there was no way they would be able to feed the cattle that day. They put a few calves into a shed—those in the worst shape—and then returned to the house.

Since there was not much they could do outdoors except worry, they turned to personal projects inside. Stan worked on his book about his life with the 24th Division in the Pacific theater during World War II, while Bob drew a few pictures, his hobby.

"I find myself drawing nothing but summer scenes," he told Stan.

The men went outside every hour or so to see that the animals had not gotten stuck in a snowbank and to mill the cattle to keep them from freezing in their tracks. They tried to bat ice balls from the noses of the cows. It seemed useless and they felt helpless. After dinner they checked the yearlings and found that eighteen head had drifted away from the corrals into a side wind.

Toward evening, when the storm seemed to have abated a little, Bob saddled up his favorite horse, Trigger, and rode south along the horse pasture fence, hoping to find the stray yearlings. He found the spot where they had crossed a snow-filled autogate (constructed to let cars cross, but discourage cattle) into a summer pasture. However, it was getting dark and his better judgment told him to go no farther on a night unparalleled in his memory.

Their radio batteries were dead and so they got the weather news by rubbering on the party line. They heard fantastic reports. Some neighbors said it was the worst storm since the three-day blizzard of 1888 and maybe even worse than that one. Everyone was nervous. No rancher thought he would come through the storm with all of his livestock alive. Some reported temperatures of between fifteen and twenty degrees below zero. Others talked of almost four feet of snow with drifts twenty feet high. Likely cattle would be found under those drifts, probably dead.

Jack Moreland called that evening to check on things. Bob reported to his father that they had everything under control as best they could, but he should expect losses.

The Morelands' neighbor, Joy C. Fairhead, telephoned next to tell of his experiences. "Dad called to warn us to stay inside," he said, "but we didn't. We put all the cattle in the best locations last night and put the yearlings in a shed near Garould's house. We checked on them in the afternoon. The shed was packed with snow and their backs were rubbing on the roof.

"We knew we had to do something. There is a closed shed in the next corral north. I asked Garould if he thought we could drive them to it. He said it looked impossible to him. I told him we would have to try or we would lose the cattle. We got them out of the first shed, shouting and whipping them with lariats to get them to head into the wind. Miraculously, they took off for the closed shed. When we got back to the house, Dad was on the phone to make sure we had stayed in. When we told him what we had done, he said, 'Don't do it again!' "

"I don't know what we'd do without the telephone," said Bob. "I can't see how the lines keep working, covered with snow and whipped by this wind."

Gene and Pauline Thurston and Lauren Dikes at the Cooley Camp pulled blankets up around their backs as they huddled near the stove. That cut off some of the numbing cold that poured into the poorly constructed house. When morning came, the blizzard still raged. The men had turned the horses into a stackyard to fend for themselves. Pauline's little pony preferred to stand by the house instead, head down and rump to the wind. If she would just huddle with the other horses, thought Pauline, she would be warmer. Gene and Lauren tried to get her to go with the rest, but she refused to budge.

Pauline scouted the house once more for food while the men followed the fence line to the windmill for a bucket of water, most of which was whipped out by the wind before they got back. She found a cake of yeast and a little flour, so she mixed a batch of dough and baked it in the oven. Gene and Lauren shook the snow off as they set down another bucket of water.

"Not much water," said Pauline. "Might be enough for coffee and maybe to wash our hands. I could melt snow."

"That's all for now," said Gene. "It's just not worth the effort. The bread you're baking sure smells good."

"It may have to last a long time," Pauline said. "That's all there is. And we have only one sack of coal."

The men went back outside to break off fence posts for fuel.

When Kenneth Hopkins and Wallace Greathouse at the Hull church finally got up the courage to go the short distance to the Noyes farm, they came back with two quarts of milk and two cans of peaches. That was enough to satisfy the children for a little while. While at the farm, Hopkins and Greathouse called relatives to let them know where they were and that they were safe.

With those six trains stalled at Kimball between Cheyenne, Wyoming, and Sidney, Nebraska, the Union Pacific Railway sent a nine-car relief train and, for a time, passengers indulged in the luxury to which they were accustomed. But during the night the water gave out and steam heat was no longer provided. Toward morning the conductor put in a call to Sidney:

"Send an engine! Our passengers are freezing."

The depot agent responded that he'd try—there was a big engine sitting in the station. Later, it managed to get through and was hooked onto the train. Then it froze up, too.

Early the next morning the conductor told the passengers to make a break for the Kimball Hotel on Main Street. The passengers struggled through several hundred yards to the hotel, followed by the train's dining car staff. Since hotel employees couldn't get downtown, the train staff took over, bringing the train's food stocks in. Even so, by evening the hotel was short of food.

Residents of Kimball who lived near Main Street brought food from their pantries. A storekeeper managed to get to his store and haul over food stocks.

"I don't know how to thank all of these generous people," said the mayor.

At Kearney, Nebraska, a passenger train stalled east of the depot, but the train managed to maintain its steam heat. It was decided to keep the passengers on board, since snow banks made it almost impossible for passengers to get downtown. However, local storekeepers managed to get sandwiches and other items to them. The enterprising circulation manager of the *Kearney Hub* tramped through belly-deep snow to deliver the latest edition of his newspaper.

At Green River, Wyoming, the telephone in the depot nearly rang off the hook as residents called offering to open their homes to stranded passengers. The pastor of the Congregational church near the depot called to say he had opened the church for as many as wanted to stay there.

The mayor helped sponsor a dance and the theater opened with a special show. Passengers said their stay in Green River was the most fun of the trip.

South of Rapid City, on the Bad River in the badlands, rancher Willard Bloom stared out the window of his ranch home near Quinn, trying to see if any cattle had come into the ranch from the north. So far, he and his son, Jimmy, had seen none.

The night before the blizzard hit, Bloom and his wife had gone to a wedding dance in Quinn. The temperature was sixty-five degrees, but Bloom felt a storm was in the air. When they got home at 3 A.M., the stars were shining brightly and the northern lights lit up the whole sky. In the morning the sky was hazy and the weather acted sort of "funny." At about 9 A.M. it started to snow. Within an hour it was the worst blizzard Willard had ever known. The storm was upon them and there was nothing to do but wait. He and Jimmy fastened a stretch of barbed wire from the house to the barn so they wouldn't get lost feeding the horses in the barn. "My father and grandfather taught me to do this," he told Jimmy.

The Bloom ranch was on the Bad River in an area sometimes known as Hart Canyon, because a cowman by that name was the first settler. "In a May blizzard in 1890, his entire herd of cattle drifted over the badlands wall into Bad Creek and drowned," Bloom told his son. "I guess our cattle won't drown, but I wonder how many will live."

Bloom thought that over the years his father and he had been well prepared for storms. Their winter range lay to the north and east of the ranch and they figured the cattle would drift into the home ranch during a storm. So far the system had worked quite well. Maybe it wouldn't this time. Bloom had grown up on this ranch, riding broncs and looking after cattle. He knew that getting through a storm without loss is about the most important thing a cowman can do.

Kenneth Parrish, manager of the Hickman Lumber Company in North Platte, Nebraska, worked only a few blocks from his home. At six o'clock the evening of January 3 he started home in the fury of the blizzard. He was not heavily dressed. The snow swirled around him, got under his coat, and blotted out his vision.

Suddenly he realized he was lost and looked for any nearby shelter. A church door loomed in front of him. What if it was locked? He tried the door. It opened.

He had hardly entered when someone else came in behind him. ''You lost, too?'' Kenneth asked with a laugh. He recognized a friend.

''I sure am. This is terrible! I'm no more than three blocks from home.''

''Neither am I, but I wouldn't try to go out again.'' Kenneth found the telephone and called his wife, who was at home with their young daughter.

''I'm so glad you're safe,'' she said at once. ''Don't

A house near Rawlins, Wyoming, is barely visible under mounds of snow.

try to come home. The house is already nearly snowed under. There's a big drift in front. I can't see across the street.''

After a few minutes a couple walked into the church carrying a sack of groceries. Soon nine persons had found a safe haven there. When the pastor learned of their plight, he told them to make themselves at home.

There wasn't much to eat. They found some crackers, bread, and coffee. Those who had groceries shared what they had. They had only one problem: they couldn't find a can opener. Kenneth and a young man found a stove poker in the furnace room, jammed it into a can of fruit, and made enough of an opening to work with. Sleeping on church pews was not comfortable, but it was better than going out into the blizzard.

Marvin and Norma Thinnes, who lived on a farm eight miles southwest of Cozad in central Nebraska, watched the snowdrifts grow higher and higher. They were worried. She was due to give birth to their second child and Marvin could see no way to get her to the hospital.

Dairyman Lester Hess, in Gordon, Nebraska, milked his cows and then dumped the milk into the snow. He had no way to get it to town.

5

January 4. . . .

AT 7 A.M. WILLIAM ADAMS, at the hotel in Seneca, Nebraska, heard a steam engine roar into town. He looked out to see snow flying in a huge arc as a rotary snowplow advanced, stopping short of the stalled trains. Dr. Carothers stepped from a boxcar hooked behind the engine, an oxygen tent and satchel in hand. When Adams ran out to help carry the doctor's equipment, he noted a small kerosene heater next to a kitchen chair in the center of the car.

"You came up in that?" asked Adams.

"Not bad at all," laughed the doctor. "This is a far better trip than many I've made in a Model T Ford over dirt roads. Where's the man with pneumonia?"

"I'll show you."

Carothers examined Miller, who was now breathing with great difficulty. He fixed the oxygen tent over him and gave him medication. Early the next morning, when Miller seemed sufficiently recovered to travel, he was loaded into the nearest coach. The

A rotary plow driven by a locomotive opens tracks that look hopelessly blocked.

engine was hooked onto the coaches and the stranded passengers were taken back to Broken Bow. It would be many days before they would break through that mountain of snow west of Seneca.

Buses fared no better than railroads. At Twin Springs, forty-three miles north of Boise, Idaho, a resort manager put in a call for help to the sheriff of that county. Twelve vacationers had arrived at Twin Springs on January 1. New Year's Day had been beautiful. The skiing was great and the twelve were having a glorious time. Then the storm struck before they could return home. They could have surmounted the twelve inches of snow that fell, but a snowslide buried both the bus and the resort. The sheriff put the problem in the hands of a road engineer, who called the resort manager. There wasn't much food on hand because the resort depended on frequent service from Boise.

"Can you open the road?" asked the manager. "We're buried under a snowslide. After our food is gone we'll have to resort to eating elk meat. I know that's illegal, but we're getting hungry!"

At St. George, Utah, Antone Prince put in a call to his pilot. "I'm worried about Wayne Gardner. He hasn't come back from his sheep camp. Let's fly over the camp as soon as possible and see if we can get his attention. That is, if he even reached the camp."

Sitting by the fire in their office near Philip, South Dakota, Georgia Jipp and her father discussed those impossible snowbanks in front of their hangar. It was 11 P.M. The blizzard had stopped. Now the doors were hidden behind ten-foot high drifts. In the middle of the runway was another huge drift that would prevent further progress once a plane got out of the hangar.

"There's no way to get a plane out without heavy snow removal equipment," insisted Georgia. "I'm sorry for those ranchers who have been calling for flights home, but there's nothing we can do. . . ."

She heard a scraping and the sounds of men's voices and ran to the door. Looking outside, she saw a brigade of seven men in broad-brimmed hats and sheepskin coats scooping snow away from the hangar doors.

"It's no use, fellas. Go back to the hotel. There's no way you can get that plane out of there without a bulldozer, and there's no dozer within miles."

"Go back to sleep, Georgia," a rancher called. "Just be ready to fly in the morning."

But Georgia and her father did not prepare for a morning flight. "Maybe we should," she told him. "They looked determined enough to do it. They're desperate."

She turned the radio on to get the latest weather information and heard a report of the blizzard that had raced across South Dakota. Now, three days later, Kirk T. Mears, Pennington County agent, was reporting a total of thirty-eight inches of snow with winds of from sixty-three to seventy-three miles per hour and temperatures well below zero.

Mears proclaimed this the worst storm in the state's history. Meteorologists had predicted only light snow. Fooled by this report, these seven ranchers had come to town for supplies and now couldn't get home. They had already tried saddle horses, but had to give up. Horses just couldn't make it around or over the drifts. It was too far to walk home. The men were distraught over the plight of their families at home and the distress of their livestock without feed.

Georgia stretched out on the office easy chair and

went to sleep.

A bright sun came out Wednesday morning at the Moreland ranch north of Merriman, Nebraska, but high winds were causing a severe ground blizzard. A bank of clouds came up about 9 A. M. from the north, and it started snowing all over again. For a time it looked to Bob Moreland as if it it would be about like the day before.

Bob helped his brother pull out the drag sled and load and scatter a couple of loads of hay to the cattle. The cattle, young and old, looked pretty bad, but as soon as they had water and hay they began to perk up. It was hard to find a decent place to scatter the cottonseed cake, and the hungry cattle shoved their noses through the snow to retrieve chunks.

"I'll go look for the eighteen missing steers while you finish up," said Bob.

He saddled a fresh horse and headed across the snow, locating the trail of the steers. They had crossed over two snow-packed auto gates and were in one of the pastures belonging to neighbor Clyde Weber. Clyde had told him over the phone that he had pulled one Moreland steer out of a snowbank the day before. Bob gathered up the steers and took them home. They were gaunt and coated with ice.

In midafternoon Weber walked into the Morelands' home to borrow a shovel. "There's a cow stuck in a snowbank and I can't pull her out," he explained.

"We opened a new pasture of bunched hay for our cows before the storm. When it started to snow we drove them into the hills, where they weathered the blizzard. However, six cows drifted south to the railroad right-of-way and mixed with Cole's cows."

Later, Joy C. Fairhead called Bob to report his losses. "I know it's too late to tell you now," he said, "but be sure to water your cattle before feeding. Garould and I fed them first and we lost several head to bloat. We took pocket knives and opened their bellies at the flanks to let the gas out. Even so, we lost several head.

"We found one cow that had tried to go over a drift and had become tangled in barbed wire. Coyotes found her before we did and chewed a hole in her thigh ten inches wide and three inches deep. We loaded her onto the haysled and took her to the barn, where we've been feeding and watering her. But I don't think she'll make it."

Toward morning Merton Thompson, stuck north of Gothenburg, Nebraska, felt his car begin to rock. He wondered if he was losing his mind. He poked his wife, Opal, who appeared to be awake. She mumbled something. He melted the frost on the window with his breath and found he could see daylight. He could also see that high winds were blowing the snow away from the car. It had been encased in snow all through the night, keeping them from freezing to death. Suddenly it began to get very cold.

"Are you all right?" he asked his wife.

"Just freezing, that's all," she replied, teeth chattering.

"We have to have help. Surely the road equipment from Gothenburg or Arnold will be along soon—if we can hold out that long." They had been in the car since 11:30 A. M. the day before, more than twenty hours.

Merton could barely see two telephone poles sticking out from a snowbank. He climbed out of the car and the wind took his breath away. He got back in.

"I'm sure there's a farmhouse a quarter of a mile north," he told Opal. "If I go find it, you won't panic and try to leave before I return, will you?"

"No, I'll stay," she mumbled.

Merton stepped out again into the racing wind. Snow swirled around him, cutting his face. That quarter-mile seemed like a thousand miles. When he finally reached the farmhouse, he found no one there. The house that he thought would be a refuge was empty. The minister who had lived there had moved away.

Merton decided to stumble on. Visibility was improving. He could see a fence line going north and what looked like a grove of trees ahead. It might be a grove of trees around a farmhouse or maybe just an old settler's tree claim. But I have to go on, he thought. Otherwise we'll freeze to death.

As he approached the trees he could make out a

large barn. Suddenly he heard a voice and saw a dozen cattle come running around the corner of the barn, followed by a dog. He heard someone yell, ''Don't just stand there, head them back!''

''Thanks be to God!'' Merton shouted back.

''Who are you? Where did you come from?'' the man shouted as he grabbed Merton by the shoulders. ''I thought you were my son.''

Merton related his plight as they hurried into the house, which belonged to the George Millers. Even before they sat down, George's wife had coffee and hot cupcakes before Merton. ''I'm not hungry,'' he said. ''My wife is in the car, freezing.''

George telephoned his son, who lived over the hill. ''Earl,'' he barked. ''Get the tractor and get to this man's car right away. There's a woman in it.''

Moments later Earl called back. ''I can't even get the tractor out of the yard. I'm heading across the fields to the car on foot with a shovel and blankets.''

Merton and George filled a quart jar with hot coffee and also headed for the car. All three reached the spot at the same time. They fed Opal the coffee and, through the efforts of all three, got her from the car. Her legs were frozen. With a man on each side, they managed to get her to the house. There Miller swabbed the frosted limbs with kerosene, relieving some of the pain.

At the Hull church in Banner County, Nebraska, where the Hopkins and Greathouse families had been shut in for two days, the women suggested that the men follow the fence line north to the William Schuebel farm. They tried, but the storm was still so severe they gave up before going far.

On Wednesday the wind subsided slightly, so they decided to try again. This time they made it, but their waiting wives did not know that. After several hours, the women began to worry. "Maybe we should pray," suggested one. "This is certainly an appropriate place."

Then they heard voices. The men were back, and the Shuebels had sent food, pillows, and blankets by a horse-drawn float. That night the families were warmer than they'd been since their arrival. They slept so soundly they let the fire go out.

When the storm subsided a little at their ranch near Chadron, Nebraska, Gene and Bob Marshall decided to risk going out to feed the cattle.

"Let's give up on the horses and just walk," suggested Bob.

Walking was all but impossible, too, they soon learned. At the Stec ranch they opened the shed where the heifers were sheltered and steam poured out. They didn't attempt to feed the animals, just shoveled the snow away from the door to give them a little air.

At Anderson Canyon they scooped a cow from her snow imprisonment. Bob put a halter on her to pull her out. Instead of cooperating, she got away before Bob could get the halter off. Later they would find it on a fence post where she had rubbed it off.

At the school section the two men drove and coaxed the cattle to a strawstack and left them to feed on their own. Nine hours later they arrived back home so exhausted they could hardly drag themselves in. It is pretty hard on a cowman to give up his horse and walk.

Alvo and Clara Crawford, living on their ranch a few miles north of Seneca, Nebraska, emerged from the house after the blizzard ended on Wednesday. He said, "It looks as if the Lord took a giant trowel and leveled the Sandhills. Only the tops are showing. In between everything is snow."

For the past two days, the Crawfords had given the milk cows nothing but cottonseed cake. This morning when he went to the barn to milk, Alvo found them with their backs nearly to the roof of the barn. Underneath them was packed snow. He and Clara dug a tunnel through the snowbank in front of the barn door to let the cows out to water. Then they took twenty washtubs of snow from the attic of their house.

According to the information Alvo picked up on his shortwave radio, North Platte had had winds of fifty-six miles per hour continuously for the past sixty hours. The temperature had gone as low as seventeen degrees below zero.

Alvo's nephew to the north had more troubles. His

Pilot Don Higgins of Ainsworth perches on the chimney of the Lester Goodrich home south of Ainsworth, Nebraska. The house had been buried three times since the November 18, 1948, blizzard. Goodrich was completely out of food when Higgins arrived.

house was almost completely drifted under. Fortunately, he had taken a scoop shovel into the house before the blizzard began. He crawled out the upper bedroom window and scooped a tunnel to the back door.

Late that afternoon Alvo noticed what looked like cattle at a schoolhouse a quarter of a mile away. He walked over on the hard-packed snow to investigate. They were steers that had drifted a couple of miles south from a neighbor's herd. Their hides were caked with snow and so were their eyes. The drifting snow had scoured the hair off their rumps.

"They would have suffocated from the ice on their noses if it had been much colder," he told Clara when he got back home. "I tried to knock the ice off their eyes. It didn't work."

At the Thurston ranch Cooley Camp the storm abated Wednesday evening and the terrible wind moderated.

"What a relief!" said Pauline. She looked out at her faithful pony still standing by the house. The hair on her mane and tail had been beaten off by the storm.

The three of them, Lauren, Gene, and Pauline, rode out to survey the damage, which they knew would be high. It was much worse than they anticipated. Dead cattle were standing or lying everywhere. Ears and tails were frozen on the living. When they tried to move those still alive, they went "on the fight"— then fell down, unable to rise.

A large steer stood by a haystack fence, looking as

Approximately 150 head of whiteface Herefords belonging to Clyde Thurston drifted with the wind onto a small lake near Ashby, Nebraska. They fell on the slick ice and froze. None survived.

if he were still alive, but was frozen solid. Others were astraddle a fence, as if tied there, also dead. One cow lay with her head back, dead, eyes still open, as if begging for help, hoping to see a haystack in the distance. Many of those alive were bloated from lack of water and feed. Pauline tried to keep from crying. She had never seen such a hopeless look in her husband's eyes.

"I wonder about Dad's cows on the north side of that lake," said Gene sadly. "I sure wish he had moved them.''

The work horses had drifted with the storm to a grove of trees south of the house. They looked pretty rough, but a feed of hay hastened their recovery.

It took the three half the day just to dig out the hay-sleds and get ready to feed hay. Toward evening they fashioned halters out of tree limbs and put ropes in the mouths of the bloated cattle to make them chew in an effort to lessen the bloat by releasing air. Sometimes it worked; more often it didn't. They even sliced holes through the thin part of the flanks to relieve the pressure.

While Lauren went off to feed his cattle, Gene and Pauline dug cows and steers out of drifts. However, those still alive died soon after being exposed to the frigid air. Hungry coyotes followed them around like dogs. Pauline watched them pull hair off the frozen carcasses seeking pieces of meat.

One-third of the United States was now buried under a blanket of snow that varied from three to five feet in depth, that is, if there was a realistic way to measure it under mountainous drifts. Those ranchers who lived in the country could not get to town; those who lived in town could not get to their livestock. And town residents were running out of groceries with no way to bring in new stocks. Farmers and ranchers, most of them at least, were well stocked with food, either bought and stored in large quantities or raised at home and canned or preserved. Beef grew on the hoof and was easily available. The threat of illness, rather than hunger, was the most serious problem for those on farms and ranches. And fuel—there was no way to get more and without it, their vehicles were paralyzed.

Norma Thinnes near Cozad poked her husband Marvin awake at 3 A. M. "It's time to go," she said. The baby wasn't going to wait for better weather. Marvin struggled to get dressed and went out to make a trail with his tractor. When that didn't work, he shoveled a path all the way to the Platte River, reaching a farmhouse at six in the morning. The woman of the house called a county road crew, which came out and got Norma to the hospital in time.

6

January 4. . .

AT THE CASPER, WYOMING, AIRPORT, high on
a windy hill west of town, pilot Ray Smith kicked a
hole through the snow on the runway. Then he kicked the tires on his Cessna 170 for no reason at all except to vent his frustration. He looked at *Tribune-Herald*
reporter Chuck Morrison and ranchers Art Eagan and
Mrs. Jerry Nicolaysen, who waited patiently for his
decision.

"We've tried to take off three times and we didn't
make it," said Smith. "The only answer I have is this:
I take off alone and land on the highway east of the
refinery. You meet me there."

Without passengers, the Cessna rose slowly in the
high mountain air and disappeared over the ridge between the airport and the refinery. Morrison, Eagan,
and Nicolaysen jumped into the Jeep and followed a
makeshift trail between snowbanks to the highway.
The wind, in its vagaries, had cleared the highway
where Smith was to land and take off with them

aboard.

The two ranchers settled into the rear seat of the Cessna. Morrison piled in front with his camera and equipment, intending to capture the storm in pictures for his newspaper.

"The ground blizzard is going to make the ride rough," cautioned Smith. "Anyone going to get airsick on me?"

"I'm more worried about those poor sheepherders out there. I don't see how they could have survived at all in this," was Nicolaysen's answer.

"Just hope it isn't as bad out there as I think it is," countered Eagan. He turned to Nicolaysen. "Do you suppose we have any sheep left?"

Smith eased the throttle forward and let the engine rev up. He checked the wind and for traffic on the road. Traffic was unlikely, since there was no place to go. The storm had hit this part of Wyoming on January 2, and now the state—which was not used to much snow on its dry ranges—was covered with two to three feet, piled in huge drifts. Ranchers living in Casper worried about their flocks and herds. They had been calling pilots all night trying to arrange for flights over their ranges.

Smith let the plane rise and surge into the head wind. Quickly it rose into the frigid air that still registered below zero. The little plane fluttered but stayed on course. Morrison set his camera against the window. Just then a gust of wind tilted the plane and

Pilot Leonard Abart of Bassett, Nebraska, was lucky to find a spot to land. Sometimes pilots could not land and had to return to the airport without being able to help ranchers isolated by the storms.

the window knocked the camera against his nose. "It'll get worse," Smith warned him.

Morrison rubbed his nose and watched the landscape as the plane rose. He had expected distress, yet he was amazed at the apparent intensity of the three-day blizzard, which was likely to be recorded as the worst in Wyoming history. Below, they could see the snow drifting across the land, filling in low places and baring high ground. Disaster showed everywhere. Cars and trucks on secondary roads were all but covered with snow. A shovel stuck in the snow beside an auto was evidence that someone had tried to dig out and gave up.

"Wonder how many people are still in those rigs," asked Smith, half to himself.

They saw four cars, one oil tanker, and a truck snowed in east of Casper. Morrison counted eight cars stuck in drifts on the Muddy Bridge Road.

"It's a hundred times worse than I expected," Morrison shouted to Nicolaysen over the noise of the plane. He lifted the heavy camera to the window and continued to take pictures. The camera repeatedly slapped against his sore nose. Smith grinned a little. Eagan and Nicolaysen laughed briefly, then quickly returned to watching for livestock and sheep wagons.

"We can mark down heavy losses after this storm," said Eagan grimly, as Smith headed the plane in the direction of Douglas. Nicolaysen and her husband and Eagan had herds and flocks north of Douglas in Converse County.

"This is awful, just awful!" cried Nicolaysen. "I've already counted 150 head of horses, cows, and sheep frozen to death."

Many had died seeking shelter, any shelter. They lay in grotesque positions, feet up, heads bent backwards. Some were still standing. Those that had made it to canyon shelters were, no doubt, buried under the snow. Often a head showed above a drift. Snow mounds indicated where sheep had perished in large groups. A wisp of smoke blew sideways in the wind from a sheepherder's wagon, assuring Eagan that at least one of his herders was still alive. There was no sign of activity, but he couldn't expect the herders to be outside.

Then they did see a herder, possibly one of theirs. His back was to the wind as he watched over a band grazing thin grass on a blown-clear ridge. "Thank God!" said Nicolaysen.

This was a country of low rainfall and little snow. Cattle and sheep generally grazed the range year around. They might be brought into shelters and fed hay during calving and lambing. Now, livestock drifted with the blowing snow. Twenty-eight head of cattle were counted along a fence line north of Douglas, all dead and tangled in a fence. Had the fence yielded, they might have found shelter. Horses that had sought shelter in blind gullies found themselves trapped in twenty-foot drifts.

"There're three horses caught in a gully trying to fight their way out," noted Eagan. "Sure hope they make it."

Approximately 1,000 head of cattle were located south of Douglas along the Burlington Railroad tracks. They were moving in an easterly direction and looking for a windswept clearing where they might be able to graze. From the air, Smith's passengers watched stragglers slowly become stuck in drifts, where they would likely die. In one group Morrison counted sixteen head of cattle already frozen to death or awaiting the end mired in deep snow.

Haystacks that meant feed for the drifting livestock were hidden beneath a blanket of snow. A cowboy seeking them from the ground level would never see them. Some sheep shelters were completely covered, probably with sheep inside.

"I've had losses," Eagan said slowly on the flight back. "I believe those were my horses dead in the snow."

"We've had losses, too," replied Nicolaysen sadly. "I think that was our sheepwagon. The sheep may be dead."

"I'm sorry," said Smith.

"In this country losses are part of the cost of operation," said Eagan.

The six Union Pacific trains tied up by snowbanks in the open country between Cheyenne, Wyoming, and Kimball, Nebraska, received special treatment. They were near the small towns of Egbert, Hillsdale, and Pine Bluffs, and these villages soon ran out of food. And so, while a rotary snowplow inched its way toward the trains, plowing through drifts twenty and thirty feet high, airplanes from Lowry Field in Denver dropped food supplies. Train crews and passengers swooped out to gather packages of bread, fruit, milk, and other items. They waved a thank-you to the pilots as the planes made a final pass. From train kitchens, cooks distributed the food without cost.

Antone Prince scanned the landscape with field

glasses as he and his pilot flew low over a wavy sea of snow covering the desert country seventy miles south of St. George, Utah. Today was quiet, quiet for the first time in several days, and the sunlight reflected off the snow. The wind had cleared a space here and there, but not enough for a plane to land.

Prince was determined to find out if he could see anything of Wayne Gardner, the friend he feared was lost in the storm. This was called the Grand Wash region, altitude 6,500 feet.

"See anything?" asked the pilot.

"Not much. There's a hump in the snow there that might be Wayne's pickup. I'm hoping he walked to the sheep camp."

They reached the camp and the pilot flew low to drop a red banner. A man Prince thought to be herder Ed Harrington came out to pick it up. They circled again, and this time Harrington waved the banner, indicating all were well—or at least alive.

"If Gardner were there, I think he would have come out of the wagon, don't you?" asked Prince.

Sheep were scattered near the camp and the canvas-covered sheepwagon. Vegetation, sparse at best, was now covered with snow. Prince could see a carcass from which Harrington had peeled the hide.

"These sheep will need hay," said Prince. "I'll call the Wool Growers Association and see if we can find some."

A buried locomotive near Alliance, Nebraska

At the Cooley Camp, Pauline Thurston saddled up her little grey pony.

"Where to?" asked Gene.

"I'm going over to the Stearns ranch to see if I can borrow some groceries."

"Good idea, if you can make it."

It may have been only two miles to the Stearns ranch, but it seemed like ten and Pauline fought her way around snowdrifts and sand knolls. Her pony's short legs were not up to the deep snow, and she resisted every step she took. Pauline crossed on the frozen lake because that route was shorter, and much of the snow had blown off it. She let the pony walk on patches of snow to keep her footing.

After a while, the snowbanks became too much for the pony, so Pauline tied her to a tree and walked the last mile. At the Stearns' house she called her parents in Hyannis to tell them she was all right and to ask about her children.

"We're terribly short on food and fuel," Pauline told her mother.

Her mother was so relieved to hear from her daughter she could hardly talk. "I couldn't sleep for worrying about you folks in that old shack," said her mother. "I'll ask Russell Booth to fly out some food."

Stearns gave Pauline half a turkey and a couple dozen eggs, which was all she could carry. By the time they got back to camp, both Pauline and her pony were bushed. Pauline started a fire from the fence posts the men had broken off and began roasting the turkey.

Late that afternoon Pauline looked out to see Lee Burton and James Davis, her neighbors in town, fly over and drop bread, butter, and a sack of coal. Pauline raced out to pick them up like a child running to gather tossed pennies. In fact, she said later, those supplies were more wonderful to her than pennies from heaven.

Ruby Stufft, the rancher's wife, was thirty-eight miles from home. She paced the floor in the Ainsworth room that her daughters Vera and Evelyn had rented, "I'm going home even if I have to walk," she said with a determination that suprised even her daughters, who were used to their mother's determined ways.

"Oh, Ma, settle down and enjoy yourself. You know you can't get home in this snow," said Evelyn.

Ruby stormed out of the room and slammed the door behind her. She had been in town since Sunday, when she and her son Harold and three daughters piled into the pickup and drove the thirty-eight miles north to town. Evelyn and Vera attended high school in Ainsworth, and Dorothy was a student at the University of Nebraska.

Dorothy had taken the train to Lincoln, that is, if they train had gotten through the snow. Harold had agreed to drive the others into Ainsworth, planning to go back home Monday evening. At home was their father, who had to feed the cattle and take care of the two younger children, Butch and Lester.

The blizzard that struck Sunday afternoon prevented any return home. Not that Ruby didn't try. She called storekeeper amd friend Del Abraham at home asking him to open his store and issue her groceries. He said no. "You're not going home in this storm, and I'm not going to get you any groceries," he said flatly.

That night she was thankful Del had refused her request. While the blizzard roared on for the three days and three nights, Ruby stayed with the two girls and slept on the floor. By the end of the third day, she had a bad case of cabin fever. After she slammed out of the room, she went to the first store she came to that sold overshoes. Her old ones were shot. The storekeeper asked what she wanted them for.

"I'm going to walk home, that's what," she answered.

"Then I won't sell them to you. You stay in town where you belong."

She tried the next store. Same answer. She went back to Abraham. "If you want something to do," he said. "How about helping here in the store?"

She agreed and spent the day sweeping the floors and putting out stock. At least it killed some time.

At the same time, the county highway department had begun the laborious job of opening the roads. But that would take a long time.

Kenneth and Harriett Phipps of Whitman, Nebraska, went out to see about their livestock. Some had survived, but others were missing.

"I guess we might as well give up. It looks hopeless," said Kenneth. They were standing before a huge snowbank that had drifted over a high sandhill.

"See that steam coming up through the snowbank? Our cows might be there," Harriett pointed out.

"Let's dig," said Kenneth.

They spent half a day digging out the snow and widening the cut so the cows could lie down. The four horses on the haysled looked like an answer. "Maybe they can pull the cows out," suggested Kenneth.

The two pulled each of the cows one at a time from

Ranchers dig out a buried cow in the Sandhills of Nebraska.

the snowbank, half their herd. They fed them hay and tried to get them to water. That evening they went back to check on the animals. Most of them were dead. Some were badly bloated. Very disheartened, the couple returned home. They were just getting started in the cattle business and had just begun to build a herd. Now they would have to start over.

On their way back, they saw steam rising from another drift. They began digging and found their turkeys, which they brought home on the bed of the hay sled. At least they would live.

"We can be thankful for that," said Kenneth.

At the airport in Philip, South Dakota, Georgia Jipp was awakened by a tapping on the door.

"Come on in," invited Georgia.

"You come out," said the voice.

It was the same rancher who the night before had told her that they would be flying in the morning. Georgia stepped out to see the hangar door open and part of the runway cleared. It was 7 A. M. and still somewhat dark, but she could see this much.

"I guess you men never heard of the word 'impossible'?" laughed Georgia. "I'll be ready soon."

Georgia had no skis for the plane. She would have to take off and land on wheels. That handkerchief-size runway that had been cleared—well, she would need more than that.

"Try it," urged the rancher.

Georgia warmed up the plane's engine. "I guess I have to try," she agreed.

She made a trial run, lifted above the drifts, circled and landed. She waved to the men. "I can handle only three," she said.

The three climbed aboard, a few groceries in hand. The little Piper, built to carry four, lifted just before its nose would have disappeared in a snowbank. Georgia wondered where they could land near the ranches. "There'll be bare spots blown clear by the wind," she was assured.

An hour later they were flying over the ranches some forty miles out and there was not a bare spot to be seen, just a solid blanket of snow for miles and miles. Some houses were nearly buried under the snow, as were cattle sheds. Some haystacks were bumps under the snow, others showed a bare spot where whipping winds had cleared them. A herd of cattle huddled together behind a windbreak.

"There's my herd!" called one of the men. "That's my sheepwagon and sheep," said another.

The heater kept the cabin warm, in contrast to the below-zero temperatures outside. When they flew low over a ranch house and Georgia opened the window to wave, the cold slammed in like a blast from the North Pole. She quickly closed the window and pounded her hand on the seat to restore the circulation.

They flew over several families who ran outside to wave and yell greetings, but no one in the plane could understand what was said. Two hours later Georgia and three discouraged ranchers were back at the airport. Her father met her as she taxied to the hangar.

"Dean Parsons just called and offered his ski-equipped plane and knows a bare spot where you can land," he shouted.

Georgia immediately flew the ranchers to Parson's airstrip. He, in turn, flew the men home. That bare spot was a plowed field that would turn soft the minute a warm sun hit it. Parsons got the breaks—the wind had whipped most of the snow from in front of his hangar runway.

The blizzard had stopped by 9 A. M. at the Willard Bloom ranch near Quinn, South Dakota. Willard and his son Jimmy were ready to ride, horses saddled. They harnessed up a draft horse and tied on a couple of lariats. They could see live cattle across the creek near the cattle sheds. So far, so good. All the sheds in sight were drifted shut. The Blooms shoveled out the cattle in one shed and pulled two out with the work horse. Within minutes the cows died.

"That's not a very good start," said Willard. "Let's get another workhorse. They'll be worth their weight in gold. We'll need them to pull out our saddle horses as well as the cattle."

What few cattle they found around the ranch they put into a stack corral, the quickest and easiest way to feed them. "We have more important work to do," he told Jimmy.

They tied a singletree and 200 feet of heavy rope onto workhorses and led two extra saddle horses, then headed for the most distant ranges, where Willard was sure they would find cattle in trouble, if not dead.

How right he was. First they pulled five cows from deep drifts. Then their saddle horses became stuck in the snowbanks and had to be pulled out. Next the Blooms found forty-eight head of cattle within a two-miles radius and more in bunches, which they brought into the hay corrals. Their saddle horses, with their winter hair coats, were soon lathered with sweat, in spite of the low temperatures, worn out from the struggle. The Blooms switched to the spare mounts.

On Bad Creek they found a cow in the top of a plum tree with twenty feet of snow under her. Bloom got off his horse and walked over to her, hoping to scare her out. She went on the fight and took off after him. He just beat her to his horse.

"Anyway, she got out of the tree," said Jimmy. The losses so far? Twenty-eight head.

After breakfast Bob Moreland of the Green Valley Ranch near Merriman, Nebraska, tied on an extra horse when he saddled up to go over to the Snyders. He was sure it would be needed before the day was over. He found Ron Snyder, usually jovial and good natured, pretty depressed. His face had been frozen and he had lost sleep from worrying over their cattle.

"I took our Caterpillar tractor over to Goose Lake last night and pulled several bulls and steers off the ice, but I left several others for dead," Snyder told Bob.   The two men gathered up a string of yearling steers and turned them into a stackyard. By then Clyde Weber had arrived and the three of them rode south, going through the pasture where Snyder kept his calves. There were dead ones all over the place, some of them tangled up in the fences where they had smothered in the blizzard. Many of them had drifted through fences into a meadow, had gotten caught on the south side with no protection and perished.

"I worked all yesterday taking anything I found

Cowboy herds a cow through drifts on the Eldon Miller farm near Belmont, Nebraska.

alive to stackyards," said Snyder.

As soon as the men found a live calf, they would tie onto it with lariats and drag it out of the drifts. Snyder would then come along with his Caterpillar and haysled, load it up, and haul it to a stackyard.

That afternoon the men went south looking for Snyder cows, which were found strung out for two miles along the railroad track. One cow had gotten onto the track and they had to drag her off. She was too weak to make it over the drifts on her own. Fences had lost their usefulness; one could look for miles and never see one. Cattle walked over then on snow-packed drifts as though they weren't there.

"I hope I did all I could," said Snyder. "I sure hate to have Dad see all this." Snyder was telling no jokes nor ribbing his neighbors this day, as he usually did.

"You did what you could," Bob assured him. "We were just lucky our losses weren't higher."

As they were rounding up the cows along the tracks, Cole, who came over to help, rode up waving his arms frantically. "Get them off the track while I flag the train!"

The others stopped to laugh. "There won't be a train along for days, maybe weeks," said Clyde. Cole stopped to laugh along with them.

At last they got 350 head together, took them to water and herded them into a meadow. Then they rode back to the Snyder ranch for a belated dinner. Snyder's hired hand had been riding north in the S.

B. Lake area looking for ninety four yearling heifers that morning, but he couldn't find them. One heifer had been found in a drift, but was sixty feet from where a horse could find enough footing to pull her out.

Bob Moreland went with the hand to find her. They shoveled enough snow away from the cow so that they could tie a rope onto her. Then they used three lariats in a Y tied to both horses and pulled her out. She seemed to be all right, so they rode on, looking for the missing heifers.

At nightfall they still hadn't found them. The men rode back to the ranch and then west to Goose Lake. By moonlight they brought in the cattle that had been dragged off the lake the day before and put them into a stackyard.

Snyder and Weber were back by this time with the haysled and reported that they had picked up eight or ten calves that had been rescued from snowdrifts the day before.

"We discovered them yesterday when we saw steam coming from the small air holes in the snow," said Snyder. However, the calves looked very bedraggled and no one thought they would live.

Weber stayed that night with the Morelands. When he went to turn in, he found his bed covered with snow that had blown in around the closed window. He brushed the snow off and the next morning said he had never slept better in his life.

January 5 . . .

On Thursday, Bob and Gene Marshal of the Marshal ranch near Chadron, took off on foot to feed cattle. Cowhand Lyle was also sent on foot to the Alton Marshall ranch to the south to see how things were there. Lyle found that Alton hadn't been feeding his cattle because he was afraid to get away from the house in the storm. He had the care of 200 head, 143 of which were steers and spayed heifers running on the three eighties.

Lyle and Alton tried to feed with a hayrack, but it soon stalled on high center. Alton then hooked a chain onto a long steel gate and used it for a haysled. Later, he fastened a tongue to it and hauled sixty bales of hay.

At the three eighties they could find no cattle. After riding for several hours they found the animals had drifted into Ed Mazenac's pasture. Leading them with a load of hay on sled and with Alton driving them with his favorite horse, Smokey, they brought the cattle to some haystacks in a home pasture and headed back to Alton's house.

Lyle tried to ride one of Alton's horses home, but it balked at the huge drifts in the deep canyon. He rode back to Alton's, left the horse, and walked home. He was exhausted when he arrived, but felt better when he heard he'd be getting a healthy bonus with his next check.

Things were now calm in Ainsworth. Ruby Stufft had given up on getting to the ranch, and so she had gone to the girls' bedroom to read and nap—and stew. Then she saw Harold running up the street to the rooming house.

"How quick can you get a few groceries together, Mom?" he asked as he walked in the door. "Don Higgins is going to fly me to the ranch. He has skis on his plane."

"Please ask him if I can go along!" Ruby said.

Harold returned to talk to Higgins, then reported: "Don says no. He can take only me and small box of groceries."

Ruby sighed and returned to her book.

Young Fred Brost, assistant manager of the Dunlap ranch between Alliance and Chadron, had gone home for New Year's Day and gotten stalled there in the blizzard. The ranch manager was snowed out, too, so Fred was worried about the cattle at the ranch. He saddled up a big, rangy bay horse at the home of his parents, Christy and Ruth Brost, twenty miles north of Alliance. He rode off against the wishes of his mother. "You'll never make it through this deep snow," she warned.

She had reason for her skepticism. Fred and his father had tried to get to the ranch two days before. That night Christy called Ruth to tell her they had made it to the Morrises.

"Why, that's only three miles from here," she answered.

"I know, but we and the horses are all tuckered out. We'll try to make it back home tomorrow."

Today, the chances of making it seemed slightly better to Fred. It was only thirty miles to the ranch, but, considering the snowdrifts (some were twenty feet high), it might as well been five hundred miles. The snow was belly-deep to his horse, even on the highway, which seemed to be the best route, although it was closed.

At noon Fred reached a farmhouse, where he warmed up and rested. Halfway to the Dunlap store his horse gave out entirely, so he got off and walked, leading the horse. Every step was a struggle in the waist-deep snow, but he knew he couldn't quit. Often he had to pull and coax the big horse along.

At nine o'clock that night he knocked on the door of the Dunlap store. Roy Wade, who with his wife owned the store, opened the door. Fred collapsed on the floor. His frozen feet would carry him no farther. His heavy mittens were frozen rigid. It had taken him twelve hours to get that far, only a few miles from home.

"Take care of his horse," Wade said to a man who had been marooned there earlier, along with several others. Mrs. Wade worked with Fred, removing his frozen clothing and setting him before the fire roar-

Road cuts near Gordon, Nebraska

ing in the big stove.

Wade called Ruth Brost to tell her Fred was fine and would stay with them awhile. Ruth repeated what she had said the day before: "Thank you, Lord!"

January 10. . .

Ron Loebig and Wiley Ferguson, camped out in the Harry Estle home south of Arnold, Nebraska, had just finished chores around the farm and were eating breakfast when the phone rang. It was the mayor of Arnold.

"We're running out of food here. Can we send a

plane to get frozen food from your truck?'' the mayor asked.

''Sure, Wiley and I will help. We don't need any of it. We're well supplied here by the Estles,'' answered Loebig.

The blizzard had stopped, but the roads were completely blocked with snowbanks. Loebig and Ferguson got to the truck, shoveled a path to the tailgate, and made ready for the plane. Soon they heard it, and then watched the pilot make a perfect landing on a flat strip of snow nearby.

Ferguson and Loebig had already set out several boxes. They loaded the plane with all that it could carry. In an hour it was back for more.

''The milk is frozen, of course,'' said Loebig.

''Who cares?'' answered the pilot. ''They can thaw it out. No one is particular now.''

He waved a thank-you as the plane circled and headed back for town. Several trips later the truck was empty and the people of Arnold were eating much better.

After the storm had subsided, the Hopkinses and Greathouses were still snowed in at the Hull church in western Nebraska. The men decided to walk to the Hopkins home, arriving there about noon. After eating a good meal for the first time in several days, they called Lloyd Craton, a neighbor, to see if he could help them get their families home.

"I have a horse and I'll fix up a sled," he responded.

Within an hour Craton was there with a float made from a wooden gate pulled by a horse. The women and children got on board, were covered with a canvas, and then transported to the Hopkins home.

The next day Hopkins and a neighbor went out on saddle horses hunting for cattle lost in the storm. They met neighbor Thad McCann staggering toward them.

"Where did you come from?" asked Hopkins in suprise.

"My sister Flo and I have been stuck in the snow for days," croaked Thad. "I finally crawled out through the window."

The men took the exhausted Thad home with them and returned for Flo with a sled and team. The car was almost covered with snow and they had to dig it out before they could rescue her. They tied Flo on the sled to keep her from falling off. She was cold and also exhausted, too far gone to talk. At the Hopkins ranch they called Everett Hogan, a pilot friend. Soon he swooped down and landed on the snow. He flew Flo to the Scottsbluff hospital for immediate attention. She was soon feeling much better, although her feet were badly frostbitten.

Thad explained later, "We became stalled when we turned north from the highway to our farm. We were returning from Cheyenne, Wyoming, where we had visited a sister, Ruby Green. Luckily, we had a wool blanket and Flo had a fur coat. But all we had to eat were a few cough drops. We ate snow for water.''

''Suffice to say 'Thank you, Lord,' for all being safe through a vicious storm,'' said Hopkins.

The highway department managed to open a trail past the Dunlap store. Fred Brost's father and brother were able to reach the highway and hitch a ride with a traveling man. They picked Fred up at the store, borrowed horses from the Wades, and rode as close to the Dunlap ranch as they could get. But they still had to walk nine miles to the ranch. Fred found he had done a lot of worrying needlessly. The cattle had broken down the fence around the stackyard and were contentedly munching the hay. The foreman had not arrived, so young Fred took charge. First he broke the ice on the water tanks.

After the first blizzard ended early in January and the cattle were fed, Leonard and Bernetha Graves, who lived thirty-two miles north of Hyannis, Nebraska, and a few miles east of the Thurston ranch, had an idea. Why not rig up a snow plow and construct a runway near the house? Maybe an airplane might see it and land on it. Leonard was a pilot and could help out if he had a plane.

''Yeah, I could feed the cattle and you could fly mercy missions around the country,'' added Bernetha.

''Are you sure you could do all of that?'' he asked.

''Sure, why not?''

They went to work. Leonard gathered some lumber from inside the barn and other material and built a makeshift snowplow. They hitched up a team and scraped off a spot sufficient for an experienced Sandhills pilot to land on.

They had no more than finished it when a light plane circled overhead and landed. It was Russell Booth from Hyannis.

"I saw this strip and thought maybe you needed help," said Booth.

"Naw, we just wanted company," grinned Leonard. "But, if you need a pilot to fly errands, we decided that Bernetha could feed the cattle and I could help, that is, if you can find me a plane."

"I'll find a plane for you," Booth replied. "You can start by flying mail to ranches. There are people needing groceries and fuel, too. Folks have been a little slack in stocking up for winter."

They flew back to Hyannis where Russell and Leonard borrowed a plane from a friend. Soon Leonard was flying mail to ranches. Ten days without mail is a long time, even where mail was normally delivered only three times a week.

The snow was packed so hard in Gordon, Nebraska, that Butch Margrave used his crawler tractor to pull an auto over eight-foot drifts, taking a patient to the hospital.

Rod Paulsen, Oshkosh, Nebraska, reported they

*A rancher is dwarfed
by massive piles of snow.*

finally dug out the hog house which had been packed full of snow. All forty of their fat hogs had smothered.

Ralph Eatinger, Thedford, Nebraska, rancher, caught away from his ranch when the blizzard hit, sked pilot Don Higgins to fly him home. He told foreman Glenn Fred he saw "many miles of livestock disaster"— dead cattle.

Clifford Hunt, south of Ainsworth, Nebraska, was heading back from feeding cattle. Still four miles from home with temperatures at minus thirty degrees, his horse broke through hard-packed snow and seemed to be stuck. Hunt fished around and discovered his steed was hung up on a telephone line. He cut the wire to release him and rode home. The telephone line normally was twenty feet above ground.

Lester Hess, a Gordon, Nebraska cattleman, stretched barbed wire between steel posts planted on top of snowbanks so high they covered the original fence. He needed to keep his cattle confined. "I believe people do the impossible when they have to," he said.

7

January 15. . .

PEOPLE LIVING IN THE WESTERN STATES, especially those living on the high plains east of the Rocky Mountains, are accustomed to violent weather, whether it be tornadoes in summer or blizzards in winter.

There have been other famous blizzards, such as the one that hit Nebraska in late November 1940, catching residents unprepared. Among those was turkey grower Dick Shinn of Halsey, Nebraska. Trucks were ready to haul $40,000 worth of his birds to market the next morning. Although Shinn and his men, plus the truck drivers, worked all night trying to unstack turkeys that kept piling up in the blinding storm, most of them smothered. The trucks left empty when the roads were finally opened.

The most talked-about storm of all was the blizzard of 1888. The day began balmy and springlike. Then the blizzard struck with fierce suddenness and the temperature plummeted to thirty below zero just as children were about to leave school at 4 P.M. Some teachers tied children together with ropes and led them to a farmhouse; others kept them at the schoolhouse. Some children had already started for home before the storm hit. Many froze to death, and that is why it was called the "Children's Blizzard." Ranchers didn't put up much hay then, and cattle on the open range without feed or shelter died by the thousands.

But this winter of 1948-49 was already being proclaimed the worst in the history of the western states. Even old-timers who remembered the blizzard of '88 admitted, after thirteen days of storms, that this winter was the worst yet. The 1949 disaster covered a larger area than any other storm, stretching from Canada to Mexico, from California and Washington to the Missouri River. All or part of the states in this area suffered from the storms in one way or another. On January 15 nineteen degrees was forecast for lower California, which had already suffered a $25 million loss to its $100 million citrus crop. Residents were urged to use natural gas sparingly.

It had been traditional in earlier years for ranchers to lay in stocks of groceries and fuel for the entire winter. Roads were poor and towns a long way off. After the arrival of better roads and the automobile, many ranchers became accustomed to going to town often and felt they could get what they needed at any time.

The first blizzard, in late November 1948, hit

hardest in an area south of a line that angled across Nebraska from southwest to northeast. The second major blizzard, in January of 1949, hit hardest north of the line, with some of those living on this line getting the full blast of both, especially in northeast Nebraska and parts of South Dakota. One could draw a line around southern South Dakota, the north half of Nebraska, eastern Wyoming and Colorado, and enclose the most severe area of the storm.

Desperate for help, mayors of towns in the storm's path began asking their governors for aid and the governors in turn began asking their legislatures for funds.

Meanwhile, in South Dakota, Georgia Jipp came in from servicing her plane just as her phone rang. It was a rancher fifty miles out in need of groceries.

"How about our mail?"

"Sure, I'll bring it, if you have a bare spot for me to land," she said. "My plane has no skis. The ski-equipped plane is out."

"There's a plowed field blown clear six miles away. I'll meet you there. The snow is packed hard enough to walk on."

A rancher needing a ride home was waiting in the hangar. Georgia's mother, always helpful, had brought her sandwiches and coffee. Georgia sat down in the sunny side of the hangar to eat while her mother gassed up the plane.

A rancher, delighted and relieved to receive food supplies, heads home.

She was thankful for her mother's kindnesses. When she returned from a flight her mother was always there with hot coffee and sandwiches, which was about all Georgia had time for today, as she and her father were the only pilots in town. They flew endless hours in attempting to supply the needs of troubled ranchers. There were requests far beyond their ability to meet. There had been another blizzard since the first one, although without the same duration or intensity.

Georgia nodded, then fell sound asleep with a sandwich in her hand. She awoke with a start when her mother touched her. "Your plane is ready. Poor girl, you're all worn out," said her mother. "This is too much for you; you're a mosquito against an eagle."

The rancher awaiting a ride would have to walk nearly six miles to his home, but he was eager to go. He stood in front of her with a bag of essential groceries in one arm and was sorting through his stack of mail.

"People are hungrier for mail than for food and livestock feed," Georgia said to her mother. She loaded the rest of the groceries along with the passenger, taxied to the end of the short runway, and soon was in the air. Below was nothing but a white sea.

A few miles out she saw an SOS stamped in the snow, one of the signals people had been instructed via radio to use. She dropped low over the ranch, dipped her wing, and flew on.

As she landed on the snow-covered field, a rancher rode over the hill, his horse lathered with sweat. She awaited his arrival.

"I don't know what we would do without you pilots," he said. "We were almost out of food."

Georgia watched him tie the groceries behind his saddle and ride off, sorting through the mail as he rode, letting his horse pick his own trail. She flew on until she reached the point to to let off her passenger.

"I sure hate to leave you out here," she said.

"Don't worry about me," he answered, "I can make it. I'm just thankful to get this close to home."

A distress signal tramped in the snow is in the foreground of this picture.

Georgia hesitated to take off. She was apprehensive as she watched her passenger start his six-mile hike into a sea of nothingness. But there was a springiness in his walk that indicated he was so thankful to get home nothing else mattered.

She dropped down at the ranch where the man had stamped out his SOS.

"I'm out of cigarettes," he told her.

"That hardly qualifies as an emergency," she told him. "The next time I go this way, I'll drop a carton over your house." She hoped they would land in his horse tank.

Most calls were real emergencies and Georgia was

Nurse Gertrude Okresza and pilot Ed Swopes prepare to take off for a snowbound ranch.

glad to help. However, there were a few frivolous requests. Like the man who had called a couple of days before and said they needed a nurse. When Georgia landed on the pint-size runway in front of the house, his wife ran out and threw her arms around the nurse, exclaiming, "I'm so glad to see you, auntie!"

When she returned a half-hour later Georgia wanted to know who was sick.

"Me," said the wife. "I have a boil on my neck."

Georgia steamed a bit as she flew the "nurse" back home. One day she received word that a woman and her children "were starving and they were about out of fuel," but when Georgia landed the woman did not even come out and help carry the free food that had been sent by the Red Cross. These cases were soon forgotten among the numerous instances of great gratitude from so many others.

Georgia heard over the radio that county agent Kirk Mears had contacted representative Francis Case in Washington, D.C., for help. The South Dakota legislature appropriated $100,000 and set up an advisory committee to answer calls. The South Dakota National Guard provided bulldozers and ski planes—flying boxcars that made her little Piper look like a gnat. They began dropping feed to cattle. The first delivery was 1.5 tons of hay and 200 pounds of protein cubes to Carl McDonald near New Underwood.

This was the day that Kenneth Parrish received a phone call at his lumber and coal company in North Platte, Nebraska.

"Do you have any coal?" came from a plaintive voice.

"I have four carloads," responded Parrish.

"Can I have a wagonload if I come in?" asked the caller.

"I'll sell it on a first-come, first-serve basis. I can't do otherwise," said Parrish.

"I'll be there as soon as I can. I'm coming with six head of horses on a lumber wagon. We're desperate." He hung up without giving his name or saying where he was coming from.

With the new snows, trains were again stalled at various locations—eight at Ogden, Utah, five at Salt Lake City, and six at Sidney, Nebraska, besides numerous trains on branch lines. Six trains were held up at Omaha. The western routes were blocked.

It was the second urgent telegram the mayor of Gordon, Nebraska, had sent to his state senator, Don Hanna of Brownlee: "Could you hurry more aid? Fuel and baby food very short."

Hanna called Governor Val Peterson telling him that people were getting desperate. "In Lincoln County to the south," he said, "ranchers report cattle dying of pneumonia. Hay is up to thirty-five dollars a ton if they can find it or get to it." (Normally, hay sold for from ten to fifteen dollars a ton.)

"It is the toughest job of this sort that has confronted Nebraska in a long time," stated the governor later. "My informant from Gordon said it was the worst he had seen in thirty-five years. Fifteen-foot drifts are to be seen in all direction."

Anne Germany, living in Gordon at the time, wrote to relatives in another part of the state:

> The storm struck like a cyclone the day I was 21 and not even a brave soul ventured out of shelter for three days. People were warned by radio and telephone not to even open their doors. The first day of the storm a man came pounding on our door, exhausted. He was lost.

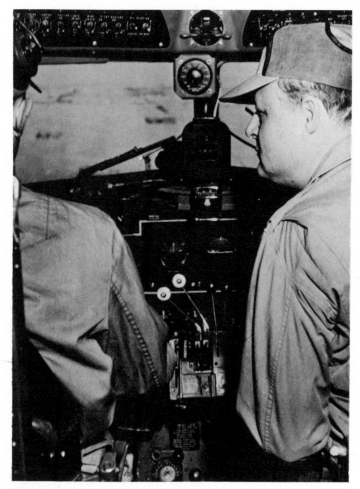

Nebraska governor Val Peterson inspects damage caused by the blizzards.

"I stepped out of our door and got lost," he said. When he came to our door he was only a couple of doors from his own house but he thought he was in another part of town.

When the 50 mph winds and blinding snow subsided, we had to climb out of an upstairs window and dig tunnels through huge drifts to get to our doorway. Many drifts were twenty to twenty-five feet high, completely covering some houses. Most families would not have ventured out even on the fourth day had it not been they were running out of food. All of us were totally unprepared for this storm. It was dangerous for older people to be out at all, for the crust over the snow gave way so easily.

Then the second emergency set in. In a few days the stores' standing stock was exhausted. There was no way to replenish it. Fuel soon gave out and power lines broke. From then on you can imagine all things that could, and did, happen. When the storm struck people either found shelter or froze to death, mostly the latter.

A dear old lady was found frozen to death [probably Harriet Brown]. Evidently she had opened the door and was unable to close it. Furnaces blew up because flues were clogged with snow and two girls of our Sunday School class burned to death.

The mayor asked for volunteers to shovel a road to the cemetery. One burial was that of the beloved black woman.

Pilots of small aircraft were rapidly becoming the real heroes of the winter. Mrs. Manes, wife of flying service operator George Manes of Ainsworth, Nebraska, wearily continued to take calls for help from farmers and ranchers in an area many miles square. She tried to keep her husband and his assistants supplied with sandwiches and coffee, about all that they would take time to eat. There were far more distress calls than they could ever handle. Finally, at midnight, when the telephone had quieted down, she wrote a letter to her mother, Mrs. George Nye, in Lincoln:

Will try to get off a few lines to you tonight. We have gone through so much since January 2. It seems like a horrible nightmare. I have been out of my mind and George is so thin his pants won't stay up. I did get him to a doctor for a checkup yesterday but the doctor said all he needed was a lot of rest and a few regular meals.

For several days running no one here has had time for anything to eat except what breakfast we took time to heat up at 5:30 in the morning. We have to get up so early in order to get the pre-heaters going to warm up engines. People are begging for help from daylight until dark. We don't take time for lunch, then when we get the hangar door shut at night the men are so tired all they want to do is go to bed rather than stay up longer for something to eat. If the boys didn't try to fly in such bad weather and stay up so late at night!

A pilot delivers supplies to a couple who had been isolated for three weeks.

One day the sun came up and warmed the snow to the extent that they couldn't take off with skis—it was too sticky. George had gone to Bassett to fly a doctor to a patient out in the Sandhills. Just before dark he called and said he couldn't take off with skis and to send Don Higgins with the Stinson which didn't as yet have skis. "Have him land on the highway," he said.

It became awfully dark and not a sign of them. Finally, I caught a glimpse of the navigation lights on the Stinson as it went down the runway. I stepped out the door to watch just as the mechanic ran past shouting, ''They just nosed over!''

I just couldn't look, I was so scared. Planes catch fire so easily when they nose over. It was Don alone. He said he landed on the wrong runway and hit a big snow drift.

On another occasion, when planes were icing terribly, George thought he had to go out and take care of someone. It got darker and darker and no George in sight. I just stood there and cried and cried.

I called Rolland Harr of the Nebraska Department of Aeronautics in Lincoln and told him we would have to have help with planes and pilots. Since then he sent three men with planes but even with them they are still going all day long as fast as they can take off and land. It has gotten to the place we just can't take care of all the calls. People in their desperation have begun getting mad over the telephone. I can understand their feelings but I can't take that kind of treatment.

I just wish you could witness these little airplanes, overloaded by about 300 pounds with food, feed, gas, fuel and coal, bouncing over a sea of drifts in some field. They take a terrible beating and, miraculously, they still fly. The people most desperate for help live in the most awful hills and inaccessible places. . . .

V. L. Munger, the fireman who helped bring in the train from Ravenna to Alliance, Nebraska, on January 2, breathed a sigh of relief. The telephone had finally quieted down and he hadn't had a service call for thirty minutes.

As soon as the first blizzard ended in early January, he had gone out flying mercy missions requested by the county board. He and a partner owned a crop-dusting air service. Their planes were in great demand for flying food and fuel to area ranchers and farmers and flying the sick to doctors. The city and the countryside shivered under a blanket of three to four feet of snow, part of it from a blizzard that had struck since the January 2 storm. That morning John Huff and Bill O'Brian took off to deliver mail to a ranch northeast of Alliance, using one of Munger's best planes.

A while later the phone rang. It was the farmer who was to receive the mail.

"We've had a terrible accident," he said. "Come at once and bring a doctor!"

"What happened?" asked Munger anxiously.

"The pilot flew low to get my attention, struck a power line, and crashed into my house. I'm afraid the men will die—they're seriously injured."

Munger called a local doctor who drove out to the airport immediately, bringing a stretcher.

"Jump in," said Munger, not bothering to explain. He hardly gave his plane time to warm up before taking off the runway. He circled the farm a couple of times and landed in a field nearby. The two raced to the house.

The first plane had penetrated the side of the house, one wing sticking grotesquely up in the air. The engine rested on the dining room table. The farmer and his wife had struggled to get Huff and O'Brian inside to keep them warm, knowing they should have been moved with care.

The doctor examined the fliers, then turned away sadly. "I'm sorry, Munger, they're both dead."

They took the bodies to the airport and called the morgue. Huff and O'Brian were the first casualties of the airlift operations in western Nebraska.

After dinner Munger settled down again in his office, hoping no calls would come; he was too depressed to accept any more. But the phone rang again. It was the local Red Cross:

"Would you pick up Joe Herian, a seventy-year-old rancher near Antioch, and deliver him to the Alliance hospital?"

"Of course," said Munger. He turned to a pilot friend, Bob Yarbrough, who had been helping fly missions in his spare time.

"Will you take this flight? I'm so bushed I don't think I could make it and I'm too depressed over losing these good men. Take one of our new Cessnas."

Less than an hour later the phone rang again. It was Yarbrough, his voice apologetic. "I landed all right," he said, "but after I took Herian on board and tried to take off, I lost control and wrecked the plane. I sure am sorry, V. L."

Munger called to his partner asleep in an easy chair. "Let's take two planes down. I guess Yarbrough

Two pilots were killed when their plane hit a power line and smashed into the side of a farmhouse near Alliance, Nebraska.

didn't have enough experience flying on skis. The snow is getting soft in this warm sun.''

At the ranch they picked up Yarbrough and Herian. Then Munger, too, had difficulty getting off in the soft snow. Yarbrough continued to apologize. ''You did all right,'' reassured Munger. ''You saw that we had trouble, too.''

Munger was sorry only because the wrecked plane was so badly needed. Then Arthur Johnson, who lived near Berea, called. ''I'll offer my plane and services,'' he said.

''Thanks, Art,'' said Munger, ''this has been the worst day in my life. I can use your help.''

Antone Prince, sheriff at St. George, Utah, paced the floor of his office. He called his pilot. Would he fly him over Gardner's sheep camp again?

''Sure. Meet me at the airport in an hour.''

Prince was appalled at the snow cover as they flew low over the sheep camp. A lump of snow under which he knew Gardner's truck to be buried had grown larger. There had been another blizzard since the first time they flew over. This time, when they buzzed the Gardner camp, two sheepherders came out, but no Gardner. It was apparent that Gardner had not reached camp. The sheep were scattered over a narrow area nearby, trying to pick sparse grass sticking above the snow. The herders waved them on, indicating no serious problem. But Prince could see there was a problem for the sheep. There were numerous dead ones scattered around; a few had been skinned, the hides spread out on the snow. The sheep needed feed badly. However, his chief concern was: what about Gardner? Surely he was not still in the pickup?

Back at his office Prince called friends and organized a search party to find Gardner. He and a dozen men with jeeps and shovels started out. Late that night they reached the sheep camp and, just as Prince suspected, there was no Gardner. They worked their way back to the pickup under moonlight and dug it out. No Gardner. Prince would order hay for Gardner's sheep to be dropped from aircraft as soon as possible.

Kirk T. Mears, from his county agent office in Rapid City, called his state representative. He advised him that the winter had been a disaster for many people:

> Few rural people are able to move even in their own yards or to contact neighbors. Telephone lines, surprisingly, remain intact but are available to few people.
>
> Sheds are drifted full, either locking cattle inside or preventing them entering. Some herds moved with the storm, some against fences, and some drifted into deep ravines where they perished.
>
> The snow is so deep saddle horses can't travel and haystacks look like eggs in a great saucer. Hand-shoveled paths are soon erased by winds which never

get below twenty MPH.

County and state highway crews work day and night to open roads. They have hired men with extra equipment but it is a losing battle. Private pilots bring in requests for help from ranchers who need trails to haystacks.

Mears' representative called back immediately, saying, "We want you county agents to help coordinate relief efforts. We are going to send as much help as we can."

Pauline Thurston looked out the door at the Cooley Camp when she heard a plane overhead. She ran outside as it buzzed the camp and landed nearby. It was Russell Booth of Hyannis.

"Hop in, Pauline, and I'll take you to town so you can see your kids, get a few groceries and some coal," he said.

Once in the air, Russell buzzed her husband Gene who was loading a stack of hay and then swung south to Hyannis.

"Look down there on Hibbeler Lake," said Russell.

Pauline did and the beauty of the day disappeared. There, scattered over the lake, lay the dead bodies of 150 head of cattle—the ones that Gene had suggested to his father be moved away. They were covered with snow, with a head or a leg poking up here and there. Coyotes tore at the frozen hides.

"That's the worst sight I've ever seen!" shouted

Pauline over the noise of the engine. "Dad Thurston was going to move them the next morning after the storm started. Now he has only the hides left."

In Hyannis Pauline found that her sister, Alma Edelman, was not only babysitting her own three children and Pauline's four, but her home had become a refuge for many half-starved, half-frozen neighbors who had run out of food and fuel.

"I'd better take our children home," said Pauline. "You have more than you can handle."

"No, we're getting along fine. A few more don't make that much difference."

Russell flew Pauline to her home near Ashby. She opened the kitchen door to find a six-foot drift of ice and snow inside. The clothesline and cellar were completely covered, so she didn't try to bring up any canned food.

In a small shed behind the house was supposed to have been a sow with a litter of pigs. The sow had tramped the snow until she could get out an open window high in the wall. Then she found another shed where she and the litter survived. Pauline poured them a bucket of corn and walked back to the plane.

Back at the camp she asked Russell to drop down where Gene was loading hay. She told Gene about the cattle on the lake.

"I was pretty sure that would happen. It was natural for them to drift that way in the blizzard. I'm sorry," he said sadly.

Taylor Melvin, who operated a small ranch in northern Nebraska, described what that winter was like: "Every day is the same. You shovel out all the doors to the barn, open all the gates and scoop a path to the water tank. Every day the winds blows them shut again.

"It didn't matter whether we received a blizzard, which we did once or twice a week on the average, or we were hit by high winds, the results were the same—roads and paths filled and snowbanks higher that the day before. The digging job was just that much harder the next time."

Ben Andrick, an Ellsworth, Nebraska, rancher, had his ideas on the winter:

When we returned [on January 2] from a visit twelve miles north of our ranch, a fine snow was falling. Neither the radio nor the barometer indicated a blizzard. However, I took no chances on the weather report and corralled all the cattle. Two hours later the wind was a howling tiger, unleashing a fury of snow that defies description.

All through the night the wind and snow pounded the house. We kept two fires burning to keep warm. In spite of this, a cold draft swept through every room. Our house was insulated and had storm windows, but that fifty to sixty MPH wind combined with snow and three degrees below zero temperatures sure didn't help the heating problems.

At 6 A.M. the next morning I lit the fire, dressed

warmly and went out to milk and feed the milk cows.
By now the drifts were four feet deep. The wind and
snow struck me in the face with a thousand stinging
particles. I turned my head away from the wind and
headed for the garage and from there to the barn.
After milking I worked my way around seventy-five
range cows in order to get to the door. One of them
resented it and kicked my lantern to pieces. I saved
the milk but I lost all respect for that cow.

I planned a trip of a quarter of a mile to load hay.
That may not seem far, but was a long, long trail in
a blizzard.

I already had on the heaviest woolen underwear,
wool socks, flannel shirt, heavy trousers and shoes.
Next came a pair of overalls over the trousers and a
pair of overshoes. From the closet came a sheepskin
Army Air Force coat with a parka of the same material
edged with long fur. A pair of heavy woodchopper
mittens with wool liners completed my outfit.

I started the tractor and hooked onto the haysled,
which has a twelve-by-fourteen-foot bed. I headed for
the haystack that was only a quarter of a mile from
the house, placed for just such an emergency. Going
south to the stack was easy with the wind to my back;
coming back would be much tougher. The haystack
loomed dimly in the swirling snow and I had to investigate which side of the stack I should pull up on
to get closest to it. I placed the steel cable around the
stack.

Doing this my face had to take the blast of the wind
and snow. Ice formed on my eyebrows in a solid sheet

and the long fur on my parka became a ring of ice around my face and an inch wide. I removed the ice from my eyelashes by placing both mittens over my face and blowing upward, loosening the ice enough to come off without taking the eyelashes with it.

I mounted the tractor and sent it forward, throwing all its weight against the cable. After three tries, the hay came loose and slid onto the sled, about a ton and a half. My face was beginning to lose its feeling so I knew it was freezing.

The tractor couldn't budge the load. I lunged foreward again and again. For over an hour I worked a minute or two at a time, then ran for the side of the sled to get out of the wind and clear my eyes. The sled finally began to move and head for the corral. I fought to get my load around the last snowdrift and to the cattle. . . .

Jay Catton didn't worry about his 100 head of hogs on his farm near Wausa, Nebraska. They broke down a ring of corn stored outside and lived ''high on the hog'' all winter. They managed to break a trail from the hog house to the corn pile each day.

8

January 20 . . . .

BOTH *LIFE* AND *TIME* MAGAZINES sent reporters and photographers to record the blizzards and their consequences. *Life* stated that the January 2 blizzard originated in the Yukon Valley and traveled across Canada, then turned south, with Nebraska, Wyoming, and Colorado suffering the most. That list should have included South Dakota. Three or four major blizzards had followed that path by mid-January. Twenty-two lives had been lost in Montana because of the weather and it was estimated that the loss of livestock would reach into the thousands over the region.

Most newspapers sent photographers into the area to record the disaster. The *Omaha World-Herald* and the *Lincoln Journal* sent reporters out in small aircraft, on horseback—any way to get them on the scene. Their excellent photos appeared almost daily, recording the tragedy in progress.

Railroads had little success bucking snowbanks as they tried to rescue villages which were running out of food. The *Northwestern Newsliner,* published for employees of the Northwestern Railroad in South Dakota, gave graphic details of the struggle by that railroad:

> Rail and highway traffic has ground to a halt as snow piles up in cuts thousands of yards long and five to thirty-five feet deep. Traveling on wings of racing winds, snow is packed to a firmness not unlike concrete.
>
> Using snowplows, rotaries, and wedges, crews smashed against walls of snow and every inch was a battle. To make matters worse, the thermometer bounced around like a yoyo. For example, on January 6 it was sixty degrees above zero in Rapid City; two days later it was fifteen degrees below zero. After warm weather, the melting snow froze into solid blocks of ice that took dynamite to blast out.
>
> Trying to open roads along the Nebraska-Black Hills Division that took the brunt of the storm was a back-breaking job. As machines bit into the huge drifts, progress was measured by the foot. On top of this, the wind wheeled back and forth across the prairie, drifting roads shut, and the jobs simply had to be done over.
>
> Crews of the two divisions worked day and night, often going without food and sleep. Snowplows were smashed by the huge, hard drifts. Hand shovelers were called in to free stuck or derailed plows.
>
> As food and supplies ran low in towns served by the Northwestern, speed became the keynote. At every

An endless task for Northwestern Railroad crews—shoveling out the tracks.

opportunity trains loaded and moved right behind the snowplows.

On January 11 and 12, just as progress seemed to be made over the territory, a second blizzard almost as fierce as the first whirled down again. Again, drifts were piled up from 500 to 1,000 feet long and two to thirty-five feet deep. Never has there been so much snow in so short a time. At Chadron, the forty inches of snowfall doubled that of the '88 blizzard.

East of Stapleton in north-central Nebraska, engineer Ted Isdell advanced the throttle of his steam engine to ram the snowbank ahead. This time he was determined to free the snow-locked villages of Stapleton and Gandy, which had been completely isolated for more than two weeks. The towns were located at the end of a branch line from Kearney, 100 miles southeast on the Union Pacific Railroad. Ahead of the engineer were another big engine, a ballast car, and another snowplow.

Surely no fourteen-foot snowbank could withstand that weight and power.

But when the snowplow and the ballast car hit that snowbank, both flew into the air, spun around, and crashed into the side of the engine, shearing off the left side of the cab. The impact almost knocked Isdell out. He thought his ribs were broken. He looked over at his brakeman, E. L. "Red" Redman. The cab had torn into Red's body and Isdell knew he was seriously injured. He was also very still.

"Red, are you okay?" Isdell asked his friend urgently.

No answer. He reached over, shook him, and then recoiled. He was dead.

Isdell checked next on fireman Eugene H. Rock, who lay on the cab floor. He had serious facial cuts and a badly bruised shoulder and back. Thinking he shouldn't move Rock, Isdell decided to send to Stapleton for a doctor. Just then the engineer from the lead engine came running back to investigate. He was horror-stricken.

As soon as Dr. Carr arrived from Stapleton, riding in a four-wheel drive panel truck, he examined Rock and Isdell, laid them on a mattress in the panel truck, and took them to the nearby Walter Marley ranch. During the transfer, they were engulfed in sub-zero weather and lashed by icy winds.

At the Marley ranch, a call was put in to pilots C. O. Romans and Bob Watson in Arnold. A while later, they somehow managed to land their plane in the whipping winds and carried Isdell and Rock to the Arnold hospital.

Back at the scene of the accident, Dr. Carr pronounced Redman dead. Looking at the wreckage of metal and steel, he said, "It'll take a cutting torch to free his body. Send word to Gandy for Wesley Fowler. He has welding equipment."

Fowler set out at once with his tractor-drawn equipment and was soon stuck in a snowbank. Fowler's

A snowplow east of Stapleton, Nebraska, smashed into a fourteen-foot drift, overturned, and slammed into the second engine, killing the brakeman.

friends—Elmer Stephens, Virgil Wells, and Don Vetter—loaded the equipment into a jeep and started out again. Soon it too was bogged down. Seeing their predicament, the foreman of the Milldale ranch brought a four-horse team and haysled to them and carried the equipment to the locomotive. Working in sub-freezing weather, the men labored until midnight to free Redman's body. Ranchers in the vicinity provided food and hot coffee to the workers. It was after 2 A.M. before they reached Stapleton and the mortuary.

Another work train with equipment for clearing the wreckage left Kearney the next day but was called back after the weather forecast called for additional snow and high winds. Eventually, it took a crew of fifty men to free the train and restore service to these two towns.

Kenneth Parrish, manager of the Hickman Coal Company in North Platte, Nebraska, was surprised when he looked out the window to see a man with six horses hitched to a lumber wagon drive onto the scale. The horses were lathered with sweat and looked completely played out. The man (Parrish never did get his name), who was bundled up in a cowhide robe, looked like an Eskimo. He crawled stiffly off the wagon and came inside, throwing off the robe and hugging the heating stove.

"Need coal?" asked Parrish.

"Yep."

They went out to the coal bins and scooped on a large load. Boxes of groceries in the wagon box were secured on top of the coal. The man sat down by the stove again. Parrish was about to ask him where he was from, when the man began to speak.

"I'm the one who called about the coal a while back. I've been on the road for three days. I live about seventy or eighty miles out. Every place is out of coal along the way—Ogallala, Hershey, Paxton, all of the towns. We've been out of fuel at our house for days—we've been burning furniture and we gutted the inside of the barn.

"I couldn't get out with a team, so I walked to a neighbor and borrowed two teams from him. That wasn't enough for this snow and so I borrowed one more team from another neighbor."

Parrish tried to get him to stay for one good meal before heading back.

"No," he said. "I've got to get back as fast as I can. I'll eat some of the groceries along the way. My family is hungry and out of fuel for sure by now. I'll pay for the coal as soon as I get back to town in the spring. Some of the groceries and coal are for my neighbors, too. They are about as bad off as we are."

Parrish offered him a bale of hay. "Let's unhitch your teams, water and feed them," he said, "and let them rest a while or you'll never make it back. You make a sandwich and I'll make you a cup of coffee."

The man consented reluctantly. After eating, he fell asleep by the fire. An hour later he jumped up and said he had to get going. It was a sad and worried man who climbed atop the coal and urged his horses on.

"I wish I could do more for you," said Parrish.

"You've done all you can. Thanks." And he was gone.

Alvo and Clara Crawford, who lived north of Seneca in the Nebraska Sandhills, had gotten used to fighting the blizzards that followed each other with clock-like regularity. They had moved the stock cows to the cow camp seven and one-half miles east, where there was windrowed hay that had been partially uncovered by the ever-racing winds. Still, it took some engineering around snowbanks to get the animals there. At first the cows found the hay easily. Now, their noses were becoming sore and cracked as they dug through the snow for the feed than meant survival.

"Can't keep a good Hereford down," smiled Alvo as they watched the cows work to get to the long hay.

Every day the Crawfords had watched planes fly overhead, bringing medical supplies, groceries, repairs, and mail to neighbors. At night Alvo continued to listen to and talk with other ham radio operators. The news indicated that the winter was bad everywhere.

This morning they looked up from caking the cows to see a crawler tractor with a snowplow come over the hill. When the driver got close enough to talk, he stopped.

"I'm from the Simonson and Lowe ranch twenty miles north," he said.

"Come in and stay overnight," offered Clara.

"I'll open the road to town first and you can follow me in," he said. They did and then returned home. That night a high wind blew the trail they'd made full of snow. The day's work had been fruitless.

The storm did the Crawford's daughter Carol no good either. Her mother was the schoolteacher. Carol was the only pupil, so she had school every day.

But she fared no worse than the thirteen school children in a district south of Gordon, Nebraska, who also didn't miss a day. Their school bus stalled in a drift near the Gordon Creek Hereford Ranch and they and their teacher stayed at the ranch until February 12.

Near O'Neill, Nebraska, a pilot observed a rancher digging in the top of a snowbank with a scoop shovel. He landed to see if help was needed.

"No," said the man. "I'm looking for my windmill. I thought this would be a good time to oil it. The last time I heard it, it squeaked a little."

At our home south of Comstock, Nebraska, we had been snowed in for twenty days. Lucky for us, the five miles of north-south highway to town were kept blown free, but seldom could we get the children to school. One day our neighbor Dave Nordstrom walked in and suggested we go to town for groceries. There we heard that the Valley County supervisors had hired bulldozer operators to open township roads. Pilots from Ord had been supplying essentials to neighbors back in the hills.

Eight miles northwest of Ericson, Nebraska, Marilyn Keenan complained to her parents, Everett and Lena Keenan, that her side hurt.

Appendicitis! was the first thought that went through her mother's mind. The Keenans had been isolated at their ranch for nearly a month with no way to get out or to summon a rescuer.

"Don't worry, honey, it'll be all right," said Lena, but she exuded more confidence than she felt.

Everett felt helpless. "Our only way to a doctor is with a team and wagon," he confided to his wife. "But I don't see how even horses can make it. If Marilyn isn't better soon, that's what we'll have to do."

Leonard Woeppel of Martin, South Dakota, volunteered to fly supplies and food to distant ranchers and county agent, Kirk Mears, assigned him No Flesh Canyon in Shannon and Bennett counties.

No Flesh Canyon was deep and inaccessible, but home to two hundred families. All were now locked under huge snowdrifts, and many of them were desperate for supplies.

"I'm glad *you* got that canyon," laughed Georgia Jipp.

Woeppel grinned and mounted his aircraft. After the first trip he knew why Georgia wasn't jealous of the assignment. He had to fly down the canyon between badlands walls in order to get near enough to drop supplies to the houses. After his first trip he explained to Georgia what it was like.

"I had to hold the groceries outside the plane for quite a distance before I could drop them. Look at my frostbitten fingers!"

But for Georgia, flying was no better. In the bitter cold it took hours to warm up plane engines. The damp cold made windows frost over and so it was frequently necessary to fly with the window open and the heater off. That meant frosted fingers. She could stay in the air for no more than two hours.

Radio stations transferred emergency calls to fliers, and Georgia kept a sharp lookout for signs of distress when she was in the air. Folks would stamp a signal in the snow and Georgia would drop down to see what was needed.

Flying in such weather and bouncing the little planes over frozen strips of land was damaging to aircraft. She and others worked nights repairing damage, checking over the planes, and installing heaters to make flying more comfortable and safe. After each trip Georgia's mother met her at the gas pit with coffee. She'd service the plane and schedule the next flight— details that meant a great deal to Georgia.

It was hard to maintain a schedule. People were hungry for news and much time was taken up in conversations. From the air Georgia began to see bulldozers pushing out from town to ranches. Trails showed in the snow with canyon-like walls, wide enough for one vehicle. However, often the same trails were blown shut the next day.

Day after day Georgia watched a little calf which continued to stand near its mother's frozen body. Somehow it managed to survive.

The rescue workers were dedicated. One of Georgia's co-workers, Carl Thompson, flying out of

Helpers rush to right a plane buffeted by the wind.

Bennett, became so involved in flying food to the needy and patients to hospitals, that one day he neglected to return before the weather turned bad. At his last stop it was snowing so hard that he didn't dare take off. Later he reported to Georgia:

"I was so busy worrying about everyone else I forgot we might run out of fuel at home. So I walked home in the storm and rigged up an old stove and broke up some old furniture for fuel. My legs still ache from that long walk home.

"It took my friend Joe McChoughnhay, a rancher north of Merriman, Nebraska, to add a little spice to my job. He was out tending cattle when I flew over. He had found a bull which appeared to be sick, left his horse, and walked over to him. The bull, however, was not sick, just bloated. I watched from the air while he jumped up and chased Joe. Joe has long legs, but it was hard for him to run in the deep snow. It was a race to the windmill and, for a time, it look as if the bull might win. But Joe climbed the tower and waved me on."

Pilots located many cattle that would never have been found from the ground and reported them to the ranchers in the area. Then the ranchers could ride to them, feed them cotton cake, and lead them to shelter.

Good news finally came for the pilots. About 130 ranchers, some flying great distances, met with C. W. Anderson, division engineer of the South Dakota State Highway Department, urging him to send more help. H. C. Rampler, executive engineer at the highway department, announced over radio KOTA of Rapid City that all bulldozer owners should call the district highway office for assignments. They were to open county roads as necessary to get to the next farm or ranch, "opening only one haystack per unit until all have been reached."

With money going out at two hundred dollars per hour for road clearance, it didn't take Pennington County long to run out of money.

Hay for Utah livestockmen was being shipped in from Montana. Antone Prince, St. George sheriff, called Douglas Clark, president of the Utah Wool Growers, for more hay for Gardner and other sheepmen.

"We're being threatened with an embargo by Montana livestockmen because they're running into a shortage at home," answered Clark. "Flying over the area, we've sighted eleven other ranchers snowbound and surely in need of hay and supplies. The situation is getting critical."

Reports continued to come into Prince's office. A Mr. Trimble had been without food for two weeks. Prince ordered supplies air-dropped to him. Each morning Prince checked with Vernal Gergeson, chairman of the emergency livestock committee, to prod him for hay and other feed. Each morning this committee met at Salt Lake City to allocate hay for that day on the basis of individual need. Planes or four-wheel-drive trucks delivered it.

Reports coming Prince's way indicated that the distress was widespread. Two herders, Ronnie Miller and Rass Larson of Heber, who had been taking care of 2,000 sheep for Fitzgerald Brothers Co. of Eureka, had been reported missing for two weeks in the Tintic region southeast of Salt Lake City.

A report from Iron County, north of St. George, an area only recently opened to cultivation and grazing, indicated forty-two inches of snow was piled up

As soon as roads were opened in Utah, hay was trucked in for starving cattle.

in twenty-foot drifts. Roads to this rail station had been blocked for seven days, with a lone telegraph line the only communication with the outside world. Supplies were running low at the Beryl community.

Prince was sure that it would be impossible to reach the snowed-in ranchers for some time, even if the roads were opened soon. Many of them had contracted for feed with valley farmers, but there was no way to bring it in.

Cattle caught in the blizzards were either lost or buried on the ranges. C. R. Burns, who operated 2,000 acres raising polled Durham cattle, told Prince that he had been able to reach only part of his cattle. He was worried that losses in the district would run to sixty percent. Burns had appealed to Utah governor J. Bracken Lee, who promised help.

John Anderson of Cedar City reported to Prince that he was opening roads to isolated ranchers and their range camps for more than two weeks. He wrote, ''These men report that they have been unable to find more than half their livestock and many of those rescued were too weak to be driven to range feedyards. The toll is expected to reach into the thousands of head of cattle and sheep.''

Newspaper reporter Athena Cook wrote about a sheepherder who carried 350 pounds of hay on horseback to his sheep every day. ''Old-timers don't talk about pioneer hardships so much anymore,'' she concluded.

In mid-January pilot Bill Harrison of Granby, Colorado, flew his light plane to Rock Springs, Utah. When he returned, the weather turned bad and he had to land on an isolated plateau north of Vernal. There he spent a week without food in minus-forty degree weather. Pilot Jim Skaridge and D. C. Lebeoutillier found him on January 20, alive but badly frostbitten. They flew him to Grand Junction, Colorado, to receive medical treatment.

Evan Reid, 35, of Soda Springs, Utah, owned a snowplane equipped with an engine and a rear propeller. He and his wife decided to have some fun with it and went to visit his brother-in-law, Harley Wood, about ten miles north of town. Two miles from Wood's place the snowplane overturned.

"I'll walk to Harley's for help. You stay here," Evan told his wife.

The next morning Wood, awakened by his dogs barking, went to investigate and found Reid's body. Knowing about Reid's snowplane and, suspecting his sister might be in or near it, he went in search of her.

Wood quickly found the snowplane and nearby he found his sister with her arms locked around a fence post, unconscious. He pried her from the post and took her home. Her legs and arms were frozen. When she recovered she told her story:

"I waited in the snowplane for several hours and then decided to follow the fence line. First, I tucked my dog under my coat. When I could go no farther, I locked on that fence post. I'm sure my dog kept me from freezing to death."

Robert Ottum, *Salt Lake City Tribune* reporter and photographer, thought it would be exciting to take some pictures. The excitement went out of the venture when he and seventy-five other motorists stalled near Bigham in a snowstorm. Soon their autos were covered with snow. They stayed in their cars and hoped for the best.

When the weather quieted, Ottum slipped an old rag around his ears and crawled out of his car. His auto was equipped with a two-way radio, and he became the contact point for the others, notifying relatives and even calling doctors for medical aid.

When they were rescued two days later, Ottum helped carry infants to the end of the line, where police vehicles were waiting. He also got some excellent snow pictures.

Storm relief headquarters in Cheyenne, Wyoming, received a call from John Hay, Jr., in Rock Springs, over 200 miles west. Speaking for the Wool Growers of Sweetwater County, in the southwest corner of the state, he said, ''Ranchers here have about one day's feed supply on hand and we're getting desperate.''

The office manager answered that Union Pacific officials were indefinite about when they could get the lines open out there. ''There has to be a way,'' thought Hay. He called the Union Pacific superintendent in Cheyenne.

''I have an idea,'' he said. ''We have ninety-two cars of feed on track sitting there. How about rerouting them through to Denver, and then to Salt Lake City by way of the Denver and Rio Grande? From there they can be put on the UP to Ogden, Utah, and from there taken to Rock Springs.''

It took a while for the superintendent to digest all this. He made a few calls and sent off some telegrams. That afternoon those feed cars were on their way, although they would travel three times farther than normal.

Hay called his neighbors to give them the good news, reminding them, ''We still have to get the hay to your livestock. We have snowplows ready to start as soon as the feed gets here. Trucks can follow the snowplows and all of us must be ready to help.''

Three days later the cattle were being fed.

The director of the Wyoming Game and Fish Department put out a call for volunteers to help feed starving animals. ''There is serious danger of game being depleted,'' he said. ''Antelope, drifting onto roads and rail tracks, have been killed. We estimate 400 to 800 head have been killed by trains. One truck killed 400 head in one bunch. We have estimated a twenty-eight percent loss of antelope. It may run as high as ninety percent in the Red Desert region.''

He was surprised at the response. By afternoon men were at his office with offers of toboggans, snowsleds, and airplanes. By evening some antelope were eating hay dropped from the air, and toboggans pulled by halftracks were getting close to other herds.

In order to accommodate the immediate needs for rescue and relief, Wyoming governor A. G. Crane appointed R. J. Hofman, a Cheyenne businessman, as coordinator. He was to be assisted by Red Cross officer Harold M. Brown. Fred L. Warren, a leading stockman of southwest Wyoming, and Col. R. L. Esmay, the state's adjutant general, were requested to fly over the area. Warren had already seen heavy losses to his flocks and herds.

When the men returned, Warren reported, ''We saw beneath us only a vast sea of snow. Fences are completely buried, and in many instances just the roofs of ranch houses and the tops of windmills are showing.''

Governor Crane called a special session of the legislature, making an appeal for funds. They voted $200,000 for relief, and if more was needed, they would add another $500,000. Each county board was instructed to appoint one member to serve as chairman and coordinator of the relief effort. Most county treasuries were already empty.

The governor laid down priorities: first, attend to the medical cases. Second, deliver food and fuel to families. Third, open roads to livestock separated from their feed.

Then he called the Civil Air Patrol. Some 300 members and other private pilots responded almost immediately. They were ready to fly.

The Mountain States Telephone Company's little snowbuggy was being used to skim over hard-packed snow and render emergency services. Near Cheyenne it took three expectant mothers to a hospital, where two of them gave birth within an hour. In another case it was used to rescue a stranded motorist and deliver him to his snowbound family. On its return trip it picked up two college students who had been marooned in their car for sixty-two hours without food or heat. They were close to death when they were rescued and taken to a hospital. Another urgent call took the snowbuggy five miles from Cheyenne to bring in a college professor whose feet were frozen.

Radio became the great communicator. Announcers transmitted messages such as: "Residents living four miles south of Torrington are in dire need of fuel and food. Will the nextdoor neighbor please make an effort to help?"

The response was usually, "Yes."

Near Chadron, Nebraska, Benton Marshall, put in a call to pilot Frank Snook. "Can you fly me to town? I want to meet with the county commissioners."

"I'll be out. Take me about an hour." Benton was relieved when he saw the plane land on the snow near his house.

"We need help pretty bad," he told the commissioners in town. "Neighbors are running out of food and fuel and some are running out of livestock feed. The *Chadron Record* reports there are sixty families in the community who have been isolated since the January 2 blizzard.

"But what can be done and who will do it?" asked a commissioner helplessly.

"How about the U. S. Army?"

"I'll call the commanding officer at Lowry Field near Denver," said the chairman.

The commander was skeptical. Benton asked to speak with him. He recounted their experiences for the past three weeks and that of their neighbors. Final-

A rotary snowplow clears a portion of the nearly 4,600 miles of state highways in Wyoming blocked by the storms.

ly the commander agreed to send two weasels (army halftracks) and six personnel to operate them.

Benton asked the Chicoine brothers, local machinists, about building toboggans to be pulled behind the weasels. "I don't know how much we'll accomplish; there are drifts forty to fifty feet deep in some of our canyons," Benton told the machinists.

In western Nebraska a trail finally was opened to allow Merton and Opal Thompson to go home, but not directly. They drove south to Gothenburg, east to Cozad, north to Broken Bow and then on north to Anselmo, double the normal distance. There they found their son Duane stacking eggs in the corner of the kitchen, gathered from his mother's 350 laying hens. They had survived.

Then came another blizzard that stopped all activities. It seemed that winter would never end.

9

January 25. . .

ON JANUARY 24, 1949, President Harry S.
Truman put into effect "Operation Snowbound," a
massive rescue operation involving many states. It was
an attempt to save millions of sheep and cattle from
starvation. He asked Congress for $500,000 and
declared an emergency, naming Maj. Gen. Lewis A.
Pick, deputy commander of the Fifth Army, to head
the project. General Pick immediately sent forces into the storm area from east to west. He was well supplied with equipment and men; before the blizzard
he had been assigned the job supervising construction
of four dams on the upper Missouri River and had
begun assembling equipment and supplies for this
project.

Twelve flying boxcars were sent from McCord Field
in Washington state with orders to fly to San Fran-
cisco on Sunday and be ready to move immediately.
They were to fly to Fallon, Nevada, fifty miles north
of Reno, to take on six tons of alfalfa and other hay

A flying boxcar drops supplies to stranded ranchers in the Nebraska Sandhills.

per plane. From there they were to fly to Ely, close to the Utah border, to pick up stockmen who were to show pilots the most strategic spots to drop hay. One thousand tons of hay were alloted for the operation in Utah and Nevada. Many ranchers said they had not seen their sheepherders nor their flocks since January 2.

That same morning twelve C-82 flying boxcars flew low over a ninety-mile stretch near the Utah-Nevada border. At rooftop heights, bales of hay fell from the planes to sheep below. Wires snapped as bales hit the ground and hungry sheep ran to the feast. "Bombar-

Army crews loading a C-82 flying boxcar

diers,'' lashed to the planes with ropes, sat on the floor and shoved the bales out with their feet on a precision signal from the flight deck.

In Alliance, Nebraska, General Pick set up a headquarters for his army. Another force, moving in from the east, had already begun operations out of Ainsworth in northern Nebraska. The Omaha headquarters of the Fifth Army announced 296 pieces of equipment ready for action. Either in transit or being loaded for immediate delivery to snowbound areas were 280 drift-busting vehicles—everything from bulldozers to jeeps to weasels.

Bad weather hampered all aid efforts. Said historian Luise Love: "Vicious blasts blew incessantly with wind velocities from thirty to seventy-eight MPH, averaging around fifty-five. Temperatures hovered a few degrees below zero at all times. January 2, 1949, will go down as the first day of the worst winter in the annals of Wyoming. Storm followed storm."

Antone Prince was again out with his pilot looking for ranchers in need, as well as for his friend Wayne Gardner. He saw a large flying boxcar sweep low over the Gardner sheep camp sixty miles south of town. As it did, bales shot out the door and landed near the sheep.

"Let's circle the camp after they leave," suggested Antone.

The cargo plane made a circle, dropping more hay. Prince and his pilot watched fascinated as the hungry sheep scampered toward the bright green alfalfa. The weaker ones staggered, but found the hay, even though they were pushed back by the more aggressive ones. Sheepherders stood and stared as the plane made another pass over the flock. One of them, probably Harrington, waved his red flag in a salute and thank-you to the fliers, then ran to inspect a handful of hay as though he had never seen such a thing before.

"That is the most beautiful sight I've ever seen," said Prince. "Now if we could find Gardner alive, it would certainly be a most beautiful day."

Army and navy planes dropped 100 tons of hay and 5,000 pounds of food to Indians on the enormous Navajo Reservation in parts of Arizona, Utah, and Colorado. Truck caravans set out with food, fuel and medicine to the settlement of Araibi in Arizona, the oldest town in the area. Traders told operators that 300,000 Navajo sheep would die or be crippled. Operation Snowbound would be much too late for many sheepmen and their flocks.

Twelve counties in eastern Wyoming were formally designated a disaster area. In addition, General Pick was authorized to extend his operation into parts of Charles Mix and Bon Homme counties in South Dakota, just north of the Nebraska line.

Nebraska governor Val Peterson had earlier asked his legislature to appropriate $500,000 for emergency aid to persons in the blizzard-battered counties, saying, "I won't ask for aid from Washington until the legislature makes funds available and we have attempted to help ourselves."

However, by this time, he was ready to accept federal assistance—the job was too big for any state alone. He said, "Nebraska is suffering the greatest disaster in her history. It is costing us $240 a day on a round-the-clock basis. We need 300 bulldozers immediately plus all the rotary and V-type plows we can get."

Twelve states were officially included in the storm area: Nevada, Texas, New Mexico, Montana,

Army personnel with a weasel, a life-saver for cattle and ranchers alike.

California, Nebraska, South Dakota, Colorado, Wyoming, Utah, Arizona, and Idaho. Six states were given emergency designation—all of Nebraska and Utah, plus parts of Nevada, Arizona, Wyoming and South Dakota. The deepest snowfall recorded during the month was 134 inches at Steamboat Springs, Colorado, and all of it was still on the ground. Colorado officials declared that the month had had the worst series of storms in its history.

Benton Marshall flew back to Chadron to aid the weasels which had arrived from Denver. On this one day they delivered fuel and supplies to twenty-five ranch families. Some said these men were the first out-siders they had seen in thirty days.

Over the radio or by telephone, Chadron area residents were instructed to tramp large Roman numerals in the snow to indicate needs: I, medicine or II, serious illness. The letters to use were F for food, L for stove fuel, and C for coal.

"That weasel is a marvelous piece of equipment," Marshall told his family after he had ridden one to his house.

His son Slim, who lived with his family away from the ranch headquarters, had run out of stove oil and had resorted to burning fence posts in the old cast-iron cookstove. In desperation, he bucked snowdrifts with a team and wagon to reach neighbor Chub Thomas two miles away and bring back some oil. While he was struggling toward Thomas' house, a weasel left a thirty-gallon drum of kerosene in his front yard.

"At least you won't run out so quickly," consoled his father.

Pick headquarters at Alliance sent out bulldozers that began opening roads, many of which blew shut as fast as they were opened. The Fifth Army moved into Wyoming on January 26. Progress was slowed by high winds and drifting snow. Col. R. L. Esmay and Fred Warren sent out instructions to ranchers by radio and telephone, notifying each of them when their routes would be opened and asking them to have sup-

Supplies being dropped near Egbert, Wyoming

plies and livestock feed ready to follow the snowplows. Esmay had already lined up a convoy of forty trucks.

The Tenth Air Force, using C-47s (D-C3s) and other aircraft, began dropping tons of feed to starving cattle and sheep.

Stories of lucky survivals and intense hardships filtered out. Several Coloradans were safe after spending thirty hours in nine snowbound vehicles east of Laramie, Wyoming. A few hours after getting stuck, driver Mike Duetsch approached Ray Ryskowski in his truck.

"I kept my heater going until I was about out of gas," said Duetsch. "Can I join you?"

"Sure, why not? You can help us keep warm," said

Ray. But the engine froze about 4 P.M. and they were without heat until they were rescued.

Two men left early in the morning to clear the Midwest Road near Casper. When they didn't return, another crew was dispatched to look for them. When no word was received of the second crew, another crew was dispatched. A pilot who was sent out next found all three trucks stuck in a snowbank not far apart. Finally, using shovels, the crews made their way through.

Stark drama was being enacted across the land as hungry livestock began receiving much-belated feed. The smell of hay brought by truckers through bulldozed alleys in the snowdrifts made weakened cattle rise to their feet and charge blindly in the direction of their dinner.

In South Dakota, Rapid City *Journal* reporter Bradley Slack rode with a feed truck as it followed a new bulldozed trail: "Small calves and yearlings plow through barbed wire, tearing off clumps of hairs, or dive into crusted snowbanks, often floundering as the hay is brought to them," he wrote. "This is the drama taking place as the huge state and federal relief program fans out across the mountains and prairies."

No one could be more pleased than Georgia Jipp to see the cargo planes dropping hay and supplies to ranchers. Now she could take a nap with a clear conscience.

Caravan of hay trucks bringing much-needed aid to marooned farms and ranches north of Rawlins, Wyoming.

The Everett Keenans of Ericson, Nebraska, knew they had to do something for their twelve-year-old daughter Marilyn. She screamed with pain and held her side. It was becoming more obvious that she was suffering from appendicitis. His mother put cold packs on her side, which seemed to bring relief.

Three to four feet of snow was piled up in high drifts around their house. Because of its location, it was nearly covered with snowdrifts. After every snowstorm Everett had dug a path out from the house before he fed the cattle. It would be filled in by the next storm and the banks on each side of the path became higher.

However, their larder was well stocked with most essentials, including lots of home-canned fruits and vegetables. There was plenty of fuel, and tall cotton-woods grew nearby. Although they were only eight miles from Ericson, they hadn't been to town or off the ranch all winter, except to visit with their neighbors.

Now Marilyn was seriously ill. The time had come for action. She must be taken to the hospital. Greeley, Nebraska, was the closest accessible town with facilities. Neighbors offered to help.

"We can take her in a wagon," suggested Everett. "That's all we have. We can put hay in the bottom and cover her with robes."

This was agreed. Everett brought out his feed team and hitched up. He put in a sack of feed for the horses and Lena fixed sandwiches and a jug of coffee.

They scouted around snowdrifts and shoveled when they had to. It was hard going from the start and the horses had to be rested often. Their sweating sides heaved as they caught their breath during each stop.

The men seldom stopped to rest, especially when they heard Marilyn moan under the blankets. It was snowing now and a strong wind was whipping the snow in their faces and covering the blankets in the wagon. And the temperature was certainly below zero.

Evening was coming on as they approached Highway 281 north of Greeley. The highway had been cleared, but snow was drifting back in the road. After six miles the horses gave out completely. It was still fifteen miles to Greeley.

They stood in the leeward side of the wagon and discussed the next move. But, just as they did, they saw an oil transport coming from the north. Driving was Fred Worm.

"Get in and get warm," he offered. "I'll take you to town."

It was crowded in the cab and Everett held Marilyn on his lap. Her pain had not lessened.

In two miles the truck stalled in a snowbank. The road, which had been opened by a Fifth Army bulldozer, had blown shut. It was now five o'clock. The weather was turning into another blizzard with temperatures well below zero.

"We have to find shelter," said Worm. "I think there's a ranch not far down this road. We have to try to reach it."

The men took turns carrying Marilyn and Lena struggled along behind. Her legs were freezing and refusing to function. At last they reached the Rolland Dunning ranch.

The Dunnings hurried to make Marilyn comfortable and then treated Lena's frozen legs. The side of Everett's face was frozen. The Dunnings' telephone did not work and there was no way to let people know where the Keenans were. Lena cried and prayed.

The next morning, soon after daylight, a small plane landed on the snow. It was Ellis Carson flying a two-place Piper Cub. He was known as the biggest pilot in Nebraska at 275 pounds.

"I was sent out to find the truck driver when he didn't come into Greeley. But I can haul only one passenger," he said. Marilyn had such a fear of flying that she refused to go without her mother.

"With my size, the plane won't handle more than one passenger. You'll just have to go alone, Marilyn. Come on, it'll be all right," Carson urged.

"I'm too scared," cried Marilyn.

Disgusted, Carson said, "I'll go back to Ord for a larger plane."

Dunning put ice packs on Marilyn's side and Lena continued to pray. The she heard the sound of an airplane. It landed and in walked Walter Koinsan from Goose Lake. He had a larger plane. A daughter of the Dunnings spoke up at once. "I'll fly with you, Marilyn."

That afternoon she was operated on for acute appendicitis. Meanwhile the Dunnings worked on with Lena's frozen limbs. "We're going to have to get you to a doctor, that is all there is to it," said Dunning.

A loud banging on the door of our screened-in porch awoke us at two o'clock in the morning. In fact, it sounded more like someone trying to break it down. I arose and dressed hastily. Who could be visiting at this time of night with us snowed in and the temperature at minus ten degrees? The noise increased as I walked to open the door. There stood a man, maybe six feet tall, well-built, yelling like a maniac and showing me his hands. My first thought was that he was crazy or drunk. I came close to slamming the door shut; I wasn't at all sure I should let him inside.

"Just look at my hands!" he said holding them up for me to see. Then I could see they were frozen solid. They had kept him from opening the door and walking right in.

When I helped him in, he fell across the kitchen floor. Irene, my wife, heard the commotion and came running. "My gosh, I thought someone was beating you up," she said. "I'll help you get him into the rocking chair."

We assessed his damages. His lower limbs were frozen to the knees, and his arms were frozen to the elbows—solid. All we could think of to do for him was what we had been taught for years—pack his limbs in snow. (We were told later this is not what to do.)

"Get the washtub and bring it in full of snow," suggested Irene. "We'll put his feet and legs in that and put some of the snow in a dishpan for his hands and arms."

He quieted down immediately and gave his name as Anderson, saying that the county supervisors had sent him to see if members of the township board needed someone to open the roads.

Apparently the county had opened main roads to our community by a circuitous route, going southwest to Arcadia and then back to Comstock, twice the normal distance. The road east of Comstock, the most direct route, was completely filled with snow. We lived five miles south of Comstock and about a quarter of a mile off the road. Our township road was blocked by a twenty-foot high drift.

"I drove out and got stuck in a snowbank off the highway," Anderson said. "I saw your light and so I walked toward it; but on the way I tripped on something in your windbreak and fell. I was knocked out and lay there until I came to."

(I investigated later and learned he had struck his head on a piece of iron off an old stove.)

We had turned off the light and gone to bed at 10 P.M. the evening before, so we figured that he had lain there for four hours. "When I came to I heard your dog barking and came this way," he said.

We had heard our dog, Laddie, barking loudly all night. He seemed to be more concerned than usual. However, it was his habit to go north of the house and bark at the coyotes when they approached from that direction. I did think it strange that he stayed close to our window. I wished I'd investigated.

We worked with our visitor for a hour, feeding him hot coffee and holding cigarettes for him. As he began to thaw out, blood oozed from his skin and turned the snow red.

"We can't give him proper care; he has be taken to a doctor," said Irene. I agreed. She called his home. A short time later, at four in the morning, his wife and two friends pulled into our place, bringing the car close enough so that he could be walked to it. They were going to take him to the hospital in Ord.

Dwight Burney, a state senator, hung up his telephone at his home in northeast Nebraska after talking with one of the county supervisors in Hartington. He then drafted a letter to Governor Peterson.

"Last night's snow and heavy drifting, together with the 56 inches of snow already on the ground in the Hartington area since November 18, 1948, has made the situation desperate. All main and secondary roads are blocked and fuel supplies are running very low. Our county equipment is not able to cope with the situation. . . ."

Road commissioner Art Bond agreed with Burney. Opening roads had become a hopeless task for his inadequate equipment. One of his operators, using a D-6 bulldozer, started from the edge of Hartington at the first of the week and by Friday morning had opened one road three miles west and one-fourth mile south of town. High winds and drifting snow threatened to close it again.

Somehow, Bond had kept the road open to the Pleasant Valley store a few miles from Hartington, so that trucks could deliver supplies there. The store became a temporary post office. For several weeks rural letter carriers H. H. Johnson and Charles Huss had left mail there for patrons. Farmers struggled over snowbanks on foot and on horseback to take home a

A crawler tractor inches its way to a snowbound family living four miles west of Rock River, Wyoming.

few groceries and the mail.

The promise of assistance from the Fifth Army brought the hope of relief to pilots H. J. Gengler and Bud Becker. They had already flown fifty missions. Their most common missions were to fly groceries to snowbound families and bring back cans of cream which had stacked up. Some of the ranchers had dumped their cream in bathtubs.

"Operation Baby Lift" went into operation in Pierce County when Dr. David Ikast, a surgeon for the Lincoln National Guard, was flown in. He was presented with a schedule of seventeen babies to be delivered in the next twenty days, with most of the expectant mothers snowbound.

January 28 . . . .

A Fifth Army bulldozer crew came by the Dunning

ranch northeast of Ericson, Nebraska, opening roads again. Behind it drove the Fifth Army commander. Dunning ran out to hail him.

"Can you get a woman with frozen legs to the St. Paul Hospital? She's in a great deal of pain."

The commander asked the operator to open a trail to the house and helped load Lena Keenan into his car. His job was to open roads but, seeing her suffering, he rushed her to the hospital.

The surgeon gave her pain killers to ease the pain and worked to remove the frost.

"May I call the Ord hospital?" she asked.

When the call got through she found out that Marilyn's surgery had been successful. Then she spoke to her daughter. "How are you?" she asked.

"I'm fine," Marilyn responded. "How are you?"

"The doctor says I'll recover with perhaps a few less toes. We can be thankful we both survived!"

January 30. . . .

We also called the Ord hospital, to check on our "guest." A nurse informed us he was doing fine, that he would lose only the tips of some toes and fingers. "But he suffered very much as the feeling returned. The pain killers didn't work well and we had to tie him to the operating table to control him. You folks saved his life."

As the bulldozers and rescue equipment spread out across the western states, Congress, seeing the need for more more funds, voted another $3 million, and the president gave General Pick a blank check. Pick called it his greatest challenge since building the Ledo Road during World War II. "We are maintaining a continuous aerial reconnaissance over the area," he said. "In addition we are obtaining information from every other possible source."

Pick later reported to President Truman that in eleven days, 5,700 men with the help of thousands of volunteers had opened 32,900 miles of roads, which gave access to 69,000 people and 1,500,000 head of livestock.

In addition to the town's other problems, the water tower froze at Dwight, Nebraska (pop. 294). At least there was plenty of snow to melt for water.

In Sargent, in Custer County, Nebraska, a big bulldozer named *Henrietta* by her operators kept the area serviced. Owner Howard Saverite turned her over to Wayne Crossland and Forest Pollard, who pulled a trailer filled with food and emergency rations. They, assisted by volunteers, worked all day to get to the home of a farm wife who they were told was expecting. When they got there she said she was not due for another month and refused to return with them.

"I guess you don't win 'em all," said Crossland.

Henrietta became a hero around this village which had received forty-four inches of snow so far. Rescuers

Opening a road near Alliance, Nebraska

found disaster at every turn—babies crying from hunger and families burning furniture to keep warm. In another Nebraska community they found a woman who had been five days in her house with the body of her dead husband, unable to get help.

But Rudolf Kubic, near Stuart, Nebraska, was not so impressed with the blizzards. A bulldozer operator drove into his yard, opening a trail through deep snow. Kubic met him at his yard gate.

"Want me to open a road to that haystack?" asked the operator, pointing to a stack a quarter of a mile away.

"Hell, no. I'm saving that one for bad weather."

At Lowry Air Base in Denver, two white-coated doctors and a dozen operation officers waited tensely beside an ambulance for the arrival of Maj. Gen. Frederick Welsh from Casper, Wyoming. Finally the plane arrived, twenty-four hours late. He had flown to Casper to answer an urgent cry for help from the parents of Carol Anne Welsh, eight (no relation to the general), who was in critical condition with encephalitis. In Casper they had been grounded by a storm that was carried by seventy mile-per-hour winds. Once safely in Denver, the child was rushed to the hospital for treatment.

Bishop Nielsen, a rancher who lived eighty miles out from Casper, drove all the way into the city to see members of the Fifth Army.

"I just want to say thanks to you and to thank God for the hay. A lot of people have been thanking God and you people. Some of us would have lost eighty percent of our livestock if no help had come."

10

February 10. . . .

PARTNERS, V. TOBLER, DALE HALLAWAY, and Jack Shelm followed a snowplow into Valentine, Nebraska, and then went to the courthouse where the national guard from Fort Sill, Oklahoma, had its headquarters. The guard was there to open roads over a wide area. Tobler and his partners had been hired to drive weasels for the operation.

They sat down in a courtroom waiting for instructions, which seemed to be very slow in coming. They helped themselves to cups of coffee from a pot sitting there and waited some more.

Finally someone with the appearance of authority came in. "What do you fellows want?" he asked.

"We were hired in Omaha to drive weasels," said Tobler.

"Well, well," said the officer. He laughed and laughed. Then he left.

"I guess he doesn't think we can do it," said Halloway.

The men noted that the whole side of the courtroom

was one big map. With nothing else to do they studied it. Every ranch was represented by a pin. Colored pins showed whose ranch roads and haystacks had been opened. A man came in and moved some of the pins, showing progress.

Operators came in, picked up more cups of coffee, and went on to the next assignment. Tobler learned, in talking with one of them, that in addition to bulldozers and weasels, the guard had brought in a whole fleet of 6x6s, that is, ten-ton, ten-wheel trucks. It was apparent that the operation was well organized and doing a thorough job of liberating snow-bound ranchers.

Ranchers, with a winter's growth of beard and hair showing that they had been snowed in, were also coming into the courtroom to pay taxes and buy licenses for ranch vehicles. They were in a jovial mood, but discussed their livestock losses somberly. The sheriff told Tobler losses would run into thousands of head of cattle. Looking out the window, Tobler could see that the streets of the town had been cleaned of snow and stores were busy.

After lunch another officer came along and sat down with them. "Are you fellows catskinners?" he asked.

"Sure," they said with one voice.

"We have several bulldozers without operators. Report to the foreman for duty at once."

That afternoon Tobler began opening the highway west of town. He was instructed to open only one lane,

Two catskinners facing a mountain of snow

despite the complaints of drivers. This was not Tobler's first experience with Operation Snowbound. Earlier he had been hired at Kearney to load planes with bales of hay for dropping to hungry cattle in the Sandhills. It wasn't easy. The planes parked at forty-five degree angles for loading. The only way bales could be brought to the front was to hang onto a rope inside the plane and pull the bales foreword. In flight, when they came to hungry-looking cattle they shoved the bales out to them.

Southeast of Valentine, at Comstock, Dave Nordstrom and I were kept busy tagging along after the snowplows, helping them shovel out when they got stuck and supplying hot coffee and sandwiches. It wasn't hard for us to understand why progress was often made slowly. On level ground it wasn't so bad. They could shove the snow to one side and go on. Big drifts, such as the one north of our place, presented more of a challenge. The driver had to drive up on the snowbank, pull the snow back down, and shovel it off to the side. He might work all night on a twenty-foot drift. The operators seldom stopped for rest. After grabbing a few hours sleep, they'd be right back at it.

More heart-rending stories came in. A family of ten near Verdel in northern Nebraska had been snowbound since November 18, 1948. They were out of food and fuel when rescued. Their horses had frozen to death near the house and their cows were starving. They refused to be "liberated," so rescuers left fuel and food and arranged for feed to be brought in for the cattle.

A survey of thirty-two planes that had worked in the rescue operations in Wyoming revealed they flew 1,955 missions, remaining in the air for 1,595 hours. They landed in the most unlikely places—on the side of a mountain near Buffalo, for example, to pick up a woman suffering from appendicitis. Another plane landed on a narrow, wind-swept ridge to rescue a man with frozen feet.

Fifth Army bulldozers rescued seven families and a schoolteacher snowbound at an oil company camp in the mountains at an altitude of 7,335 feet. Though

Deep weariness shows in the face of George Kruml of Ord after three weeks of fighting the heavy storms.

only fifteen miles from Medicine Bow, they didn't see the town for fifty-two days.

"Our greatest worry was the health of the children, as getting a doctor was out of the question," said Mrs. Larsen. "Three army weasels reached camp with supplies in February. Needless to say, we were hysterical with relief. The weasel returned with a woman suffering from an ulcerated tooth. Then the army dozed a trail to the Albert Irene ranch with feed for livestock. After that we had a road out of camp to Medicine Bow."

State veterinarian Dr. G. H. Good said additional losses among livestock could be attributed to septicemia resulting from freezing limbs and to bloating following feeding after so many days of starving. Many bulls became sterile because of frozen testicles.

The Cheyenne Office of Agricultural Statistics placed losses at 41,000 head of cattle and 154,000 sheep.

A radio reporter flew to a ranch in South Dakota to see how a ranch family was doing. The rancher told him he was nearly out of feed for his cattle. His chickenhouse had been covered with snow, so he dug down to the roof and broke a hole in it to feed them. The announcer could hear the chickens clucking contentedly below.

A twin-engine Beechcraft of Nebraska's Air National Guard cruises over frozen rangeland.

February 12. . .

Tobler was working a long way west of Valentine, Nebraska, to open roads that had been blown shut the day before. He saw a man on the south side of the Niobrara River waving and hollering for help. "I'll come over on the ice," yelled Tobler.

The ice wasn't as solid as Tobler thought. Slowly the big crawler tractor sank. Tobler shut off the engine and raced to the rear end to jump off on shore just as the machine settled under the surface.

"I'll send someone up the other side," he called to the rancher, "after I hitch a ride back to town."

At headquarters the commander snorted and called for another operator in the area to get there as quickly as he could to pull the tractor from the river. Tobler went back to help. The river was not very deep, but the national guard had a tough time pulling the tractor out.

"I guess that'll convince the general that we aren't capable of running his equipment," he told Shelm and Hallaway glumly that night.

Everett Keenan followed a bulldozer out that had arrived at his ranch north of Ericson, Nebraska, that morning. At St. Paul he picked up his wife and they returned to Ord to pick up their daughter Marilyn, who was now quite recovered from the appendectomy. Lena Keenan had recovered from her frostbitten limbs as well as could be expected.

"What a joy to be home safe and well," exclaimed Keenan as they drove into the snow-covered yard. "Even those snowbanks look good now."

A private plane dropped down at the Joe Klimek farm northwest of Elyria in Valley County, Nebraska. The pilot found the family without food or fuel. Klimek, paralyzed from a previous injury, was in need of medication.

Glen Auble, chairman of the relief committee, called

Walls of packed snow remained along highways for weeks after the blizzards.

the national guard, which started out with a truckload of supplies to Klimek. They fought drifts until the truck stalled. Then they lugged a thousand pounds of fuel and food on their backs a half-mile to the hard-pressed family.

Pilot Ed Swopes of the Ord Civil Air Patrol was called to fly insulin to the Sindelars living in Jones Canyon twenty miles north of Burwell. He couldn't find a landing spot so Burwell druggist K. K. Kull, who flew with him, tied the precious insulin to a piece of red bunting and tossed it from the plane. It landed right by the windmill in the yard.

"Perfect!" shouted Swopes.

February 15. . .

It looked as if the winter was almost over in Utah. Antone Prince had little hope of finding his friend Wayne Gardner alive. But again he called his pilot.

"Let's make another flight over Gardner's sheep camp."

"I'll meet you at the airport."

Flying low over Gardner's pickup they could see that the warm sun had cleared some of the snow from it. Not far from the pickup truck, Prince spotted a hat in the melting snow.

"I'm sure that's Gardner's hat," said Prince. "Let's go back and return with a jeep."

That afternoon Prince and other men found Gardner's body. Apparently he had collapsed shortly after leaving the truck. Gardner would be just one of many who had given their lives for their flocks and herds during that terrible winter.

A man in a pickup truck pulled onto the scale of the Hickman Lumber Company in North Platte, Nebraska. He jumped out and approached Kenneth Parrish with a big grin.

"Need more coal. And I want to pay for the coal I got back in January. Remember me and the six-horse team? That coal kept us and our neighbors from freezing.''

''Sure, I remember you,'' said the surprised Parrish. ''I'm sure pleased you made it through in good shape.''

Near Merriman, Nebraska, a Fifth Army bulldozer finally freed Stan and Bob Moreland's pickup truck. It was driven to the ranch and to stacks of hay still almost buried under snow. Dad Moreland drove up from Merriman bringing supplies and groceries. ''Well, Stan, now you boys have seen a real blizzard,'' he said.

''Yes, but I guess that goes for all three of us,'' Stan answered. Stan was thinking of the many times his father had told of the blizzard of '88, which had lost out to the blizzard of '49 as the worst in history.

V. Tobler and the general from the Oklahoma National Guard returned from a trip in the country early that morning after staying overnight with a rancher from Brownlee. The day before the general had asked Tobler to take him out on an inspection tour. Fearing they might get lost, he hired a local cowboy as guide.

Even Tobler was shocked at what he saw. Cattle sheds were packed full of snow. Snowdrifts were as high as the windmill towers, even up to the fans in places. At the ranchhouse where they spent the night, snow was up to the top of windows around the house,

Wyoming Highway Department's rotary plow shears a path through twelve-foot drifts west of Rawlins.

so high the men couldn't see out.

The next morning there was a knock on Tobler's door. It was the general, who had castigated him for putting that 'dozer in the river. "My little boy has had an accident and my wife wants me to come home at once," he explained. "I need someone to drive me to the airport."

Tobler was ready in a moment. The weather had turned foggy, but the plane was able to land. "Good luck, sir," said Tobler.

"Thanks, I certainly have appreciated your help in all of this," said the general. Tobler felt he had been exonerated.

A package came in the mail for us near Comstock, Nebraska. It was from the brother of Anderson, our temporary guest. In the box was a blue leather dog collar for Laddie and a set of bookends made from pre-historic mammoth tusks which he had excavated. He had thanked us earlier for taking care of his brother, saying he wanted to send us an Alaskan husky dog, but we turned the offer down, saying one dog was enough.

I still don't see how Anderson survived his four-hour ordeal. He was poorly dressed for minus-ten-degree weather. He had no overshoes and didn't even have on winter underwear.

Near Chadron, Nebraska, Benton Marshall helped coordinate the opening of roads. It had taken the Fifth Army three weeks to open 450 miles of country roads, re-open 500 miles, and blaze 2,000 miles through fields and pastures to liberate ranchers and 26,000 head of cattle. At one time fifteen 'dozers were working in the county. Sometimes the roads blew shut in the high winds and had to be opened all over again. But the job finally was completed.

Anything worthy of the name "horse" was put to work trying to get hay to the Marshall cattle. Once they hooked up Bally, a hard-mouthed horse worked infrequently, and an unbroken five-year-old gelding, named Fog. Fog kicked and broke one of Dick Marshall's fingers, and then he and Bally ran away, tearing up the harness and equipment. Dick and Lyle Marshall needed chains for a tractor at Slim's ranch. The only saddlehorses around were a palomino stallion and Topsy, a green (newly broken) mare. The stallion made no fuss when they tied the chains on the saddle, but Topsy wanted nothing to do with them. Finally they got the chains tied on her saddle but once outside she went berserk. She jerked loose, bolted over a snowdrift, ran through a four-wire fence and plunged into a snow-and slush-filled canyon. There she broke her neck or drowned.

Rendering trucks arrived to pull dead cows off the lake near the Cooley Camp and to pick up all other carcasses. To the east and north of Brewster, trucks hauled off 800 carcasses. In South Dakota rescue operators counted 1,000 dead cattle in one trip.

Time magazine again flew a reporter over the blizzard region. He called it "a great white ruin," and reported that there had been eighteen storms in twenty-seven days. Forty inches of snow still covered much of the western states, even the Mojave Desert.

On March 1 General Pick called President Truman to tell him the army's job was over; that every farmer and rancher, and every village, had been freed. He turned in statistics:

Estimated overall losses to date: $190,000,000.

Seventy-six lives had been lost fighting the blizzards,

Rendering trucks began disposing of the thousands of dead cattle on the plains as soon as they could reach the carcasses.

in storm-related accidents, and by freezing.

Some 119,000 cattle and 134,000 sheep, valued at $19,600,000, died. Another 2,725,000 cattle and 2,825,000 sheep, valued at $421,166,000, were still endangered. (The *Record Stockman,* a national livestock newspaper, estimated that 1,000,000 head of cattle and sheep would be found dead in Wyoming, Colorado, and the Dakotas. "Underestimated" would be the correct word. Ranchers don't often call their bankers or a statistician to tell them about livestock losses. A bulldozer crew in South Dakota found 3,200 head of dead cattle, an indication that offical records would fall far below actual losses.)

Crop losses were put at $108,000,000. Property damage at $10,700,000.

Damage and revenue losses to the railroads was pegged at $50,000,000.

An estimated $1,000,000 in wages was lost.

Losses drove the Western Livestock Insurance Company of Denver out of business when livestock loss claims reached $375,000.

March 15. . .

Another blizzard hit several of the same troubled states in the middle of the calving season. Weakened cows were having enough difficulty giving birth without the storm. Heavy calf losses resulted in many herds.

April 1. . .

Chinook winds hit the northern states and the snow melted as if under a blow torch. Flooding followed. Roads, gravel and plain dirt turned into a quagmire of mud. The results tied up rural people as much as the snow, except that the temperature was more moderate.

A rancher wrote to the governor of Nebraska to thank him for getting him out of the snow. ''The army got us out of the snow but it is going to take the navy to get us out of the mud."

The Prichards and their men harnessed their horses again, hitched them to the picking wagons and harvested corn, three months late. Many of the ears were dragged to the ground or buried in mud. They were thankful for what they got.

Epilogue

THE *OMAHA WORLD HERALD* gave an explanation for the freakish weather pattern of 1948-49:

> Down in Oklahoma, where the red prairies slope upward toward the distant Sangre de Cristo Mountains, a storm was being born. A great mass, hundreds of miles wide, began marching eastward across Oklahoma and Kansas. And, as it marched, it brought winds as high as 65 miles an hour.
>
> The Blizzard of 1949 was on its way.
>
> It was like a hurricane, this storm. In its center was the "eye" of calm, clear weather. Around it, revolving counter-clockwise, were whipping winds. On its lower side it brought a sodden rain and mild temperatures. On its upper side, chilled by incoming arctic air, the storm brought snow that a howling wind churned to blot out visibility and to pile it into drifts. Colorado, Wyoming and western Nebraska first felt the storm's weight. The rest of Nebraska battened down and braced itself.
>
> Then came a meteorological freak. Instead of continuing on its expected way through Kansas, the storm

turned north on a sweeping arch that carried it past the Grand Island, Nebraska neighborhood. Then the storm doubled back on itself, moving as far west as Valentine, straightened out and went off northeast, As a result, Omaha and extreme eastern Nebraska got a double dose.

The result was a crippled Nebraska. Trains were lifeless in the snow. Travelers huddled in wayside refuges or felt the spreading nuances of frostbite in snow-stalled autos. Whole towns went on short rations. The sick suffered stoically, waiting for medical care that couldn't get to them. Today's mode of living is linked to its transportation facilities. When they suffered, paralyses resulted. Even veterans of the Blizzard of '88 were impressed.

The editor of the *Northwestern Newsliner* published for employees of the Chicago and Northwestern Railroad in South Dakota also had ideas about the origin of the storms:

You can't blame the weatherman. You can't criticize his "cloudy with light snow" forecast, which preceded the January 2 blizzard. The storm pattern was far too complex.

Boiling up from the south was one storm, another came from the northwest. These storms met in mortal combat over western Nebraska, eastern Wyoming, and western South Dakota with wind velocity rolling to 60 to 70 miles per hour. In a matter of minutes snow cascaded down, blotting visibility completely.

Lashing at each other viciously, the two storms raced back and forth across the territory for the next two to four days. When the clouds cleared away the land was locked in a grip of snow that took a month to dig from under.

Rail and highway traffic ground to a halt as the snow piled up in cuts thousands of yards long and five to 35 feet deep. Travelling on wings of racing winds, snow packed to a firmness not unlike concrete. . .

Ranchers might have survived better had not the weather decided to perform terrifying sequels every few days over the next two months. There was no way to fully recover from one blizzard before the next one hit. The storms built so quickly; there was no inkling they were coming until they were upon us—in all their fury.

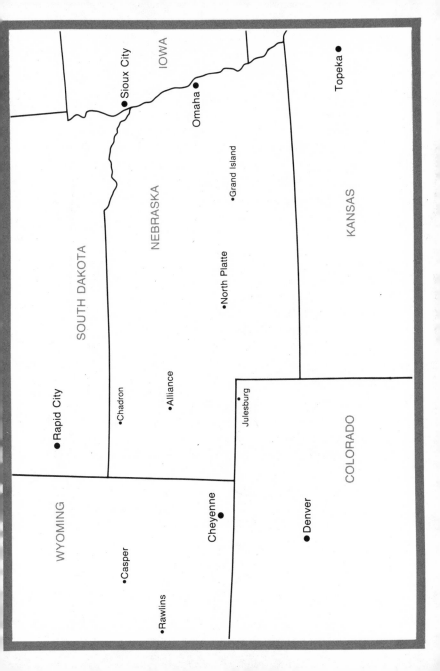

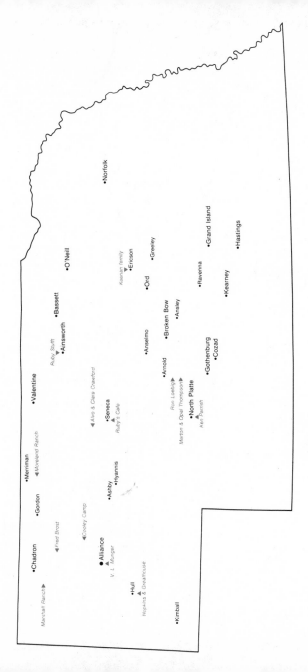

NEBRASKA

• Norfolk

• Grand Island

Keenan family
• Ericson   • Hastings

• O'Neill   • Greeley

• Ord

• Bassett   • Ravenna

Ruby Stufft   • Kearney
• Ainsworth

• Broken Bow
• Ansley

Alvo & Clara Crawford   • Anselmo

• Valentine   • Arnold   • Gothenburg
                                   • Cozad
• Seneca
Ruby's Cafe   Ron Loebig
                   Merton & Opal Thompson
• Merriman   Moreland Ranch   • North Platte
                                        Ken Farrish

Cooley Camp
• Gordon

• Ashby
• Hyannis

• Chadron

Fred Brost

• Alliance
V. L. Munger

Marshall Ranch

• Hull
Hopkins & Greathouse

• Kimball